YOUR SPIRITUAL GIFTS
CAN HELP YOUR CHURCH GROW

"The simple lesson of this book is how to identify one's gift, how to improve it and how to use it appropriately. It is a book for all Christians."
Dr. E.M. Blaiklock
Christian Challenge

Your Spiritual Gifts Can Help Your Church Grow

C. PETER WAGNER

MARC
The British Church Growth Association

This edition 1985,
Reprinted 1987
Reprinted 1990

The British Church Growth Association is a coordinating body for those interested in the growth (spiritual, numerical, organic and incarnational) of the British church today. It comprises researchers, teachers, consultants and practitioners who share information, insights, experience and new thinking through regional and national activities, a regular journal, occasional publications and other resources, seminars and conferences. It is based at St Mark's Chambers, Kennington Park Road, London SE11 4PW.

The BCGA gratefully acknowledges the help of the Drummond Trust

British Library Cataloguing in Publication Data
Wagner, C. Peter
Your spiritual gifts can help your church grow:
how to find your gift and use it.
1. Gifts, Spiritual
I. Title
234'.12 BT767.3

ISBNs 1-85424-110-9 (MARC)
0-948704-12-8 (BCGA)

Printed in Great Britain for MARC,
an imprint of Monarch Publications Ltd.,
1 St Anne's Road, Eastbourne, E Sussex, BN21 3UN by
Courier International Ltd., Tiptree, Essex.

Dedicated to
Donald and Mary McGavran
who have been precious gifts of
God to the Wagner family

Contents

Directory of the Spiritual Gifts

In this book 27 spiritual gifts are defined and discussed in some detail when each one comes up naturally in the general flow of the book. For easy reference, here are the gifts in the original order in which they are introduced in chapter 2, followed by page numbers of the places they are discussed. For additional references where each gift is mentioned more briefly, consult the index.

Preface: Why Another Book on Spiritual Gifts?

I need to make a good case for adding another book to the already too-long list of books on spiritual gifts.

None of the many books I have studied relates spiritual gifts directly and specifically to the growth of the church. Most of the books explain how the gifts help individual believers, how they bring about maturity in the church in general, and how they enhance Christian unity and brotherhood. These are good emphases, and I will make them myself, but that is not the primary focus of this book. This book is task oriented. It sees gifts not as ends in themselves, but as means toward an end. My intention is clearly to show how spiritual gifts can enable Christians to participate more effectively in the implementation of Jesus' commission to "go and make disciples of all nations" (see Matt. 28:19,20).

For this reason, some of the gifts will be stressed more

than others. While all gifts are important to the functioning of the Body in general, some of the gifts are clearly more important than others for the *growth* of the church. In the total plan of God, miracles and helps and tongues and hospitality and exhortation are highly important. But for church growth they are not as important, for example, as evangelist and pastor and missionary and apostle. During the course of the book I will mention and define 27 spiritual gifts. And even when I discuss the gifts that are secondary for church growth I will attempt to show how each can function as an aid to seeking, finding, folding and feeding the lost.

I need to point out that this book on spiritual gifts is essentially a book on church health. We who are in the field of church growth too frequently hear the criticism that we are "playing the numbers game." Or that we stress quantity to the detriment of quality. This is unfair, because church-growth leaders consistently declare that their intention is to build the Body of Christ in its full biblical sense. We are not interested in using our energies in growing religious clubs or Buddhist temples or shrines to civil religion or Kingdom Halls. But because we are interested in building and multiplying groups of men and women who are fully dedicated to Jesus Christ as Lord of their lives and who are fully committed to each other in Christian fellowship and caring, we know that church health is of vital importance to church growth. Churches grow because they are healthy. When churches are healthy they grow. Therefore, developing the dynamic of spiritual gifts in a church—because it is biblical and because it will help make Christians more Christlike and because it will enhance the health of the Body— should also help churches to grow in number.

A new book is needed, in my opinion, that picks up the strands from what has previously been written on spiritual gifts, combines them with insights developed in the church growth movement, and weaves a coherent statement showing the relationship of church growth to the operation of spiritual gifts with practical suggestions as to how this can become operative now in your church.

Previous Efforts

I began teaching about spiritual gifts over 20 years ago. A good bit of what I have been teaching has already been written and published. The first attempt came as part of a series of articles on 1 Corinthians published by *Eternity* magazine in 1967 and 1968. These were later revised and published in a book, *Our Corinthian Contemporaries* (Zondervan Publishing Company). This allowed me to lay the biblical foundation for my thinking back in the days when there wasn't much outside help.

I dealt with the subject of theological education in a book, *An Extension Seminary Primer* (William Carey Library), written with my good friend, Ralph Covell. In it I wrote a chapter, "How God Makes Ministers," in which I argued that seminaries ought to be in the business of training people who already demonstrate gifts for the pastoral ministry, rather than almost exclusively training people who have not yet discovered their gifts.

In *Frontiers in Missionary Strategy* (Moody Press), I include a chapter, "The Human Ingredient: Gifts and Call," and in *Stop the World, I Want to Get On* (Regal Books), is a chapter "Every Christian Is NOT a Missionary." These two chapters suggest that there is such a thing as a special missionary gift and show how it, along with other gifts, relates to missions.

When I studied the Pentecostal movement in Latin America I discovered that the dynamic of spiritual gifts freely operating in those churches was one of the keys to their phenomenal growth. My book on that was first titled *Look Out! The Pentecostals Are Coming*, but the current paperback is now called *What Are We Missing?* (Creation House). The chapter on gifts is, "Body Life Builds Healthy Churches."

Finally, in my first book on American church growth *Your Church Can Grow* (Regal Books), I list the use of spiritual gifts as one of the seven vital signs of a healthy church and describe how it operates in a chapter, "Let's Join Laymen's Lib!"

Although in this book, *Your Spiritual Gifts Can Help Your Church Grow*, I build on what I have written before, it is much more than a picking-up of bits and pieces and pasting them together. There is much that I want to say about spiritual gifts that I have not said previously. Furthermore, through long hours of study and numerous contacts with churches out there where the action is taking place I have learned a great deal that I did not know before. I realize ahead of time that I will learn much more after this book is put to bed, but I still feel that the time is right for it to be published. Now that people know a good bit about spiritual gifts in general, many are anxious to find out how gifts relate to specific dimensions of God's work in the world. I would like to see published, in increasing numbers, books on such topics as spiritual gifts and worship, spiritual gifts and Sunday School, spiritual gifts and social service, spiritual gifts and small groups, and spiritual gifts and you-name-it.

Where Am I Coming From?

Whenever I read a book on spiritual gifts, I like to know where the author is coming from. When he tells me that he is from the Reformed tradition, a Wesleyan, a dispensationalist, a classical Pentecostal, an Episcopal charismatic or whatever, I feel more at ease. While I know that many object to such pigeonholing, I do not, because it is difficult for me to understand a person's writing apart from the person himself or herself.

My functional and vocational orientation is that of church growth. I was converted to the church growth position when, as a missionary on furlough from Bolivia, I studied under Dr. Donald McGavran in the Fuller Seminary School of World Mission during the late sixties. Since then, church growth has become my life. I am now teaching church growth at Fuller and I also oversee the operation of the Department of Church Growth in Fuller Evangelistic Association, which brings me in contact with a large number of church leaders. Currently I am enjoying the privilege of speaking each year to somewhere around 3,000 pastors and executives from virtually every American denomination on church growth.

Ecclesiastically, I am a mongrel. My parents handed down no church tradition except having me christened in an Episcopal church as an infant. So when I became a Christian at age 19, I was on my own. Since then I have had membership in Methodist, Bible, Baptist, Quaker, and now Congregational churches. I married a Lutheran in her church. I earned a degree from a Presbyterian seminary. For the past six years I have been a member of the Lake Avenue Congregational Church in Pasadena, California, and my ordination credentials are with the Conservative Congregational Christian Conference.

As far as spiritual gifts are concerned, I do not identify with either the Pentecostal or the Neo-Pentecostal or the charismatic movements, although I have enjoyed extensive ministry among all these groups. My three spiritual gifts are teaching, knowledge and missionary. I previously thought I had the gift of administration but more recently have concluded that I do not have it. In the book I will describe how I came to understand which gifts I have and which I do not have. I have had some experience with using tongues as a prayer language, but it is not a major part of my spiritual life-style, and I will not mention it any further.

What I am saying then, is that I do not intend this to be a Baptist book or a Pentecostal book or a Lutheran book or a Wesleyan book or a Reformed book or an Episcopal book or a charismatic book or a non-charismatic book. I am not interested in polemics, I am interested in growth. I am interested in finding out how spiritual gifts can be mobilized in all the above traditions and others like them, so that greater numbers of lost men and women may be reconciled to God and brought into the loving fellowship of Christian congregations, whatever their labels. My intention is to help you see how spiritual gifts can fit into your system and make sense to your kind of people.

I know ahead of time that I will not fully accomplish this objective. Yes, I have my own presuppositions which will become obvious as the book develops. I will try to keep them to a minimum, but there are times when I will have to say that I think such-and-such a position is wrong and here are the reasons why. Some readers, I realize, will find my approach unpalatable, and will probably let me know through letters and reviews. Nevertheless, in no way is my intention to be controversial as it admittedly has been in other of my writings.

Furthermore, I hope to build what I say on what has gone before. Curiously, a few of the books I studied on spiritual gifts make much use of other authors in the field. Many give the impression that they were written in a vacuum. I myself hope to interact with other authors and stand on their shoulders. When I do, I will give credit either in the text or in footnotes. I am thoroughly impressed with the insights God has given to the likes of Stedman, Flynn, Gee, McRae, Yohn, Purkiser, and others. I need them, just as I need so many other members of the Body of Christ.

I want the book to be authentic. Therefore, from time to time, I will mention real people, real places, and real churches. Some references will be fact, some opinion. Where I felt there might be some objection, I showed the manuscript to individuals concerned and received consent from them to have it published, but with no indication by such consent that they necessarily agree with the conclusions I have drawn about them or their work. And I will also use the first person singular freely, since I want the reader to understand as fully as possible how I myself have gone through the struggles of discovering, developing, and using spiritual gifts.

My wife, Doris, has been the greatest help I have had in writing this book. Functioning simultaneously as wife and secretary, she has encouraged me at home, protected me from unnecessary intrusions, criticized the text and typed the manuscript. The efforts of Roger Bosch, my teaching assistant, in research and consultation have been extremely helpful. And finally, I need to express my appreciation to Dean Arthur Glasser and my colleagues on the faculty of Fuller School of World Mission for covering for me during this writing sabbatical and supporting me in every other way.

C. Peter Wagner

Pasadena, California
May, 1978

Introduction: The Rediscovery of Spiritual Gifts

A relatively new thing has happened to the church of Jesus Christ in America during the decade of the seventies. The third Person of the Trinity has come into His own, so to speak. Yes, the Holy Spirit has always been there. Creeds, hymns and liturgies have attested to the central place of the Holy Spirit in orthodox Christian faith. Systematic theologies throughout the centuries have included sections on "pneumatology," thus affirming the Holy Spirit's place in Christian thought.

But rarely, if ever, in the history of the church has such a widespread interest in moving beyond creeds and theologies to a personal experience of the Holy Spirit in everyday life swept over the people of God to the degree we are now witnessing. The most prominent facet of this new experience of the Holy Spirit is spiritual gifts.

It is fairly easy to fix the date when this new interest in the Holy Spirit began. The production of literature itself is a reasonably accurate indicator. As I write, I have 32 books on spiritual gifts on my desk, not counting books on the broader aspects of the work of the Holy Spirit which also have sections on gifts. Of the 32 books, 26 of them, or about 80 percent, were written after 1970. Previous to 1970, seminary graduates characteristically left their institutions knowing little or nothing about spiritual gifts. Now, only a few years later, such a state of affairs is generally regarded as a deficiency in ministerial training.

The roots of this new thing began in 1900, the most widely accepted date for what is now known as the classical Pentecostal movement. During a watchnight service, beginning December 31, 1900, and ending on what is technically the first day of the twentieth century, Charles Parham of Topeka, Kansas, laid his hands on Agnes Ozman, she began speaking in tongues, and the movement had begun. A fascinating chain of events led to the famous Azusa Street revival which began in 1906 under the ministry of William Seymour, a black pastor. And with that the Pentecostal movement gained high visibility and a momentum which has never slackened.

The original intent of Pentecostal leaders was to influence the major Christian denominations from within, reminiscent of the early intentions of such leaders as Martin Luther and John Wesley. But, as Lutheranism was considered incompatible with the Catholic Church in the sixteenth century, and as Methodism was considered incompatible with the Anglican Church in the eighteenth century, so Pentecostalism was considered incompatible with the mainline American churches in the twentieth century. Thus, as others had done before them, Pentecostal leaders found it necessary to establish new denominations where they could develop a life-style directly under the influence of the Holy Spirit in an atmosphere of freedom and mutual support. Such denominations we know today as Assemblies of God, Pentecostal Holiness, Church of the Foursquare Gospel, Church of God (Cleveland, Tennessee), and many others were formed for that purpose.

The second phase of this movement began after World War II when Pentecostal leaders saw mainline churches affected by their movement. The beginnings were slow. Some of the Pentecostal denominations began to gain "respectability" by joining organizations such as the National Association of Evangelicals. Thereby they partially neutralized the opinion held by some that Pentecostalism was a false sect somewhat in line with Jehovah's Witnesses, Mormons and Spiritists. In 1960 an Episcopal priest in Van Nuys, California, Dennis Bennett, shared with his congregation that he had experienced the Holy Spirit in the Pentecostal way, and the so-called Neo-Pentecostal movement had its start. A third important movement dates to the "Duquesne Weekend," named after Duquesne University, where, in 1967, the "Catholic Charismatics" came into being.[1]

The impact of all this began to be felt among Christians who were neither classical Pentecostals, nor Neo-Pentecostals, nor Catholic Charismatics in the seventies. While most of these Christians still show little interest in experiencing the "baptism in the Holy Spirit," the main distinguishing feature of the three charismatic movements is that they are appropriating the dynamic of spiritual gifts to themselves in a new and exciting way. Through their discovery of how the gifts of the Spirit were intended to operate in the Body of Christ, the Holy Spirit is being transformed from a doctrine to an experience. The full impact of this new development has not yet been felt in the churches of America, although there is no question that it has begun and is gaining remarkable credence. It may take until 1990 (if the Lord does not return meanwhile) for most of the implications of the total charismatic renewal to be worked out in American churches. By that time our churches may well have developed a power of ministry and growth that has been unmatched since the Great Awakenings, if even then.

How "New" Is the "New Thing"?

If my research into the part spiritual gifts have played throughout church history is any indication (and let it be said that it has not necessarily been Phi Beta Kappa quality research since the point is a minor one for me), the general picture is one of confusion. Those who are trying to prove a point by historical references are usually able to do so. Some who are cool on spiritual gifts, for example, say that many of the gifts went out of use in the churches after the age of the apostles. The intellectual center of this effort is in Dallas Theological Seminary, an interdenominational school that looks with disfavor on the Pentecostal/charismatic movement of recent decades.

John Walvoord, the president of Dallas Seminary, feels that miracles have declined in the church since the age of the apostles.[2] His colleague, Merrill Unger, writes that the fact that "miraculous charismata passed away after the apostolic period is well attested by church history." Unger argues that the miraculous gifts were given basically as credentials to the apostles for confirmation of the gospel, and therefore they passed away "when apostles no longer existed and the Christian faith no longer needed such outward signs to confirm it."[3]

Merrill Unger makes reference to Benjamin B. Warfield of Princeton Seminary who, back in 1918, wrote a book called *Miracles Yesterday and Today*. Other than the Scofield Bible, it has been the most influential book written in America against the validity of the charismatic gifts today. Warfield argues that "these gifts were . . . distinctively the authentication of the Apostles . . . . Their function thus confined them to distinctively the Apostolic Church, and they necessarily passed away with it."[4] As we will discuss in more detail later on, this point of view is strongly held on dogmatic grounds by an influential circle of evangelical churches in America today.

One of the reasons this theory of the discontinuity of some of the gifts has gained a degree of support is that not much evidence to the contrary has been gleaned from history. Warfield has not been very thoroughly challenged on his own intellectual level by scholars more favorable to spiritual gifts. But the day undoubtedly is coming. A larger company of Pentecostal scholars is now coming into its own. Undoubtedly they will begin to uncover evidence that will greatly help to clarify a situation that is anything but clear at the present time.

One of the reasons that contributions from Pentecostal scholars have been retarded is that early Pentecostals developed a strong anti-intellectualism. The ministers who set themselves in opposition to the Pentecostals and who relegated them to false cults, if not heresy, were usually seminary-trained men. Pentecostals recruited most of their ministers from the ranks of the working class on the basis of proven exercise of spiritual gifts rather than academic degrees. Seminaries were looked on with suspicion. For years there was a kind of cold war between the Pentecostals and the seminaries. But now this, for good or for bad, has largely been resolved. Both the Assemblies of God and the Church of God (Cleveland), for example, now have graduate schools which may shortly become accredited seminaries. I say for good or for bad because accredited seminaries are not by any means an unqualified blessing. While they undoubtedly will help provide scholarship for their movements, they also may accelerate the process of "redemption and lift" which can separate the churches from the working class from which they emerged. The history of the Methodist movement is example enough of how this can and does happen.

Nevertheless, Pentecostal scholars are already digging more deeply into historical records to find precedents for their emphases. I do hope that one of the things that will have happened by that nebulous 1990 date previously mentioned is that some thoroughgoing, scholarly books on the history of spiritual gifts will have been published. If so, we will all be much more enlightened than we are now by the relatively flimsy studies currently available.

What History Tells Us

In the second century both Justin Martyr and Irenaeus acknowledged that the miraculous gifts were in operation in the church. In the third century, Hippolytus makes reference to one of his writings, "On Charismatic Gifts," but the essay has never been located. In the same century, Tertullian observed with approval the exercise of spiritual gifts, and then himself converted to Montanism, a kind of third-century charismatic movement which was declared heretical by many of the mainline Christians. Bishop Hilary of the fourth century spoke of the exercise of the gifts with favor, as did John Chrysostom. The great theologian of the fifth century, Augustine, is interpreted as supporting both those who say the gifts blinked off and those who say they continued. However, James King has discovered that Augustine "completely reversed his views on miracles. Originally he disputed their continuance into his day. He later taught their present validity and claimed to be an eyewitness to some miracles."[5]

Thomas Aquinas, in the thirteenth century, considered the charismatic gifts as essential to the church, although he did not address the matter of whether they actually had continued after the apostolic age.[6] Other references to spiritual gifts between Augustine and the time of the Reformation, a span of over 1,000 years, are sparce, but undoubtedly much gold is yet to be mined by scholars who will pursue the field. It is reasonably certain that evidence will continue to build showing that charismatic gifts were operative in segments of the church in many different eras of church history.

The two most prominent spokesmen at the time of the Protestant Reformation, Martin Luther and John Calvin, had little to say about spiritual gifts. While Luther did not restrict the possibility of the use of the miraculous gifts to the apostolic age, neither did he expect them to be manifested in his churches. Calvin is generally interpreted as contending that the gifts were given mainly for the apostolic age, although he seemed to be open to the idea that they could have surfaced later on. In fact, he once included Luther among modern "apostles."[7]

The most extensive treatment of the work of the Holy Spirit between the Reformation and the twentieth century comes from the pen of John Owen of seventeenth century England. His writings were very influential in the thought of the later Reformed or Calvinistic theologians. While Owen does recognize that gifts are valid in the church, he may have been the first to distinguish between extraordinary gifts and ordinary gifts, a distinction common in later Reformed theology. Extraordinary gifts, restricted to the days of the apostles include tongues, miracles, healings, and the offices of apostle, prophet and evangelist. Similar thinking appears in such as Abraham Kuyper in the nineteenth century and Benjamin Warfield in the twentieth.

John Wesley, the father of Methodism and the subsequent holiness movements, is in a way the stepfather of the Pentecostal movement. His openness to the Scriptures and the New Testament pattern as well as his stress on the responsibility of the individual Christian helped set the stage. But, although he mentioned spiritual gifts on occasion, he was "unsystematic and incomplete in his treatment of the gifts."[8] He was so inconsistent that his direct contribution to subsequent understanding of spiritual gifts must be considered minimal.

Throughout church history marginal groups came into being which were characterized, among other things, by the use of spiritual gifts. Many of these groups were considered fanatical and even heretical by mainstream Christians of their day. One wonders whether such criticism might not have been parallel to mainstream Christian ridicule and persecution of the Pentecostals in the early part of our own century. Groups like the Waldenses, the Albigenses, the Camisards, the Jansenists, the early Quakers, the Shakers, and the Irvingites have been mentioned as using the charismatic gifts, and many of them suffered persecution at the hands of Christians who had not come to terms with the operation of spiritual gifts in their midst.

So, when I say that a new thing is happening here in the seventies, I mean just that. While charismatic gifts may have been manifested in some segments of the

Body of Christ all through Christian history, nevertheless today in America and in other parts of the world their use is more widespread. The movement crosses the boundaries of more ecclesiastical traditions, and is cordially accepted more than any other time this side of the first century, as a legitimate part of Christianity by more Christians who themselves choose not to participate.

Today's Best on Spiritual Gifts

It is probably no exaggeration to say that more literature has been produced on the subject of spiritual gifts since World War II than in the previous 1,945 years put together. And the bulk of that has come since 1971. Other than Warfield, who was writing polemics against the miraculous gifts in 1918, most of the writers before 1971 were classical Pentecostals such as Donald Gee and Harold Horton, both of England, and Myer Pearlman and B.E. Underwood of the United States.[9] The only non-Pentecostal I know of (undoubtedly there were others I have not yet heard about) who dealt favorably with all the spiritual gifts as early as 1947 was Alexander Hay, whose book, *The New Testament Order for Church and Missionary*, never enjoyed a wide circulation in the United States.

Now, as a visit to any progressive Christian bookstore will verify, the literature on spiritual gifts is prolific. There is so much on the market that if I thought this present book were to be just another general book on spiritual gifts, I would not be inclined to write it. In preparation for writing, I read 48 books on spiritual gifts, and my feeling is that we have enough for the time being. By the time I passed 20 books, I began to suspect that there is much repetition in current literature. After 48 I was sure of it.

Of the books currently on the market, some are excellent, some good, and some quite mediocre. To provide a degree of guidance, I have selected those which I consider the 10 top books on spiritual gifts. All are published in paperback and are relatively inexpensive. Almost any two or three selected at random will give you a good introduction to the field. I have indicated a couple which I feel to be of special value as a starting point. If you get all 10, you will have a solid library on the subject. If you read them all, you can rest assured that you are thoroughly up to date on spiritual gifts.

1. Bridge, Donald and Phypers, David. *Spiritual Gifts and the Church.* Downers Grove: Inter-Varsity Press, 1973. A well-balanced book from the British perspective written for a college-level audience.
2. Flynn, Leslie B. *Nineteen Gifts of the Spirit.* Wheaton: Victor Books, 1974. I like this book very much as an introduction. Flynn's approach is quite similar to mine.
3. Gee, Donald. *Concerning Spiritual Gifts.* Springfield, MO: Gospel Publishing House, 1972. This is one of the classical Pentecostal authors who wrote the book originally in 1928. Non-Pentecostals do not need to feel threatened by this book. It is profitable to all.
4. Kinghorn, Kenneth Cain. *Gifts of the Spirit.* Nashville: Abingdon Press, 1976. Writing as a Methodist, Kinghorn demonstrates how Wesleyan theology can support spiritual gifts, even though Wesley himself had a hard time handling them.
5. MacGorman, Jack W. *The Gifts of the Spirit.* Nashville: Broadman Press, 1974. Even though Southern Baptists are far from agreeing among themselves as to what attitude they should take toward some of the spiritual gifts, one of their fine scholars and seminary professors sets forth a well-balanced position here.

6. McRae, William J. *The Dynamics of Spiritual Gifts.* Grand Rapids: Zondervan Publishing Co., 1976. This is the book I most recommend expressing what could be called the dispensational/ Dallas Seminary position on the gifts. McRae writes from a pastor's heart.
7. Murphy, Edward F. *Spiritual Gifts and the Great Commission.* South Pasadena: Mandate Press, 1975. No other book approaches this one in its effort to make a direct application of the gifts to the missionary task of the church.
8. Purkiser, W.T. *The Gifts of the Spirit.* Kansas City: Beacon Hill Press,. 1975. Purkiser's small book is included because it articulates so well the position of the Church of the Nazarene and kindred spirits in other holiness denominations.
9. Stedman, Ray C. *Body Life.* Glendale, CA: Regal Books, 1972. *Body Life* can be considered a classic in the field. No other book did so much in opening the way for an awareness of the value of spiritual gifts in the non-Pentecostal denominations than this pioneer effort by Pastor Stedman.
10. Yohn, Rick. *Discover Your Spiritual Gift and Use It.* Wheaton: Tyndale House Publishers, 1974. Last (because of alphabetical order) but certainly not least. I recommend this along with Flynn as a good starting point for understanding spiritual gifts.

Notes

1. For a concise summary of the major details of the historical development of these "three streams," see Charles E. Hummel, *Fire in the Fireplace: Contemporary Charismatic Renewal* (Downers Grove: Inter-Varsity Press, 1978).
2. John F. Walvoord, *The Holy Spirit* (Grand Rapids: Zondervan Publishing House, 1954), pp. 173-187.
3. Merrill F. Unger, *The Baptism and Gifts of the Holy Spirit* (Chicago: Moody Press, 1974), p. 139.

4. Benjamin B. Warfield, *Miracles Yesterday and Today Real and Counterfeit* (Grand Rapids: Wm. B. Eerdmans Publishing Co., 1965, orig. 1918), p. 6.

5. James Gordon King, Jr., "A Brief Overview of Historic Beliefs in Gifts of the Spirit," unpublished paper, 1977. This paper is a compilation of preliminary notes in preparation for a Ph.D. dissertation on the subject at New York University. A good bit of the historical information in this section is gleaned from King's paper. Hummel's book, *Fire in the Fireplace*, also has a helpful discussion of historical evidence for the gifts (pp. 164-168).

6. See Theodore Jungkuntz, "Secularization Theology, Charismatic Renewal, and Luther's Theology of the Cross," *Concordia Theological Monthly* (January, 1971), p. 72.

7. See King, "A Brief Overview . . . ," p. 8.

8. King, "A Brief Overview . . . ," p. 14.

9. Donald Gee, *Concerning Spiritual Gifts* (Springfield, MO: Gospel Publishing House, 1972, orig. 1928); Harold Horton, *The Gifts of the Spirit* (Springfield, MO: Gospel Publishing House, 1975, orig. 1934); Myer Pearlman, *Knowing the Doctrines of the Bible* (Springfield, MO: Gospel Publishing House, 1937); B.E. Underwood, *The Gifts of the Spirit* (Franklin Springs, GA: Advocate Press, 1967).

1.
Ignorance Is Not Bliss

Who needs to know about spiritual gifts? *You* need to know about spiritual gifts if:

1. You are a Christian,
2. You believe that Jesus is your Lord and you want to love Him and follow Him in the best way possible, and,
3. You want your church to be a healthy, attractive, growing group of people showing forth God's love in your community.

"I would not have you ignorant" (of spiritual gifts) are the inspired words of the apostle Paul in 1 Corinthians 12:1. The church in Corinth that Paul was writing to desperately needed instruction on spiritual gifts. But today there are countless other churches in Philadelphia, San Antonio, Kansas City, Seattle and Nashville that need it as well. Despite a widespread renewal of interest in the Holy Spirit and His ministry in our day, church after church in America and in other parts of the world remains ignorant of this tremendous God-given dynamic for church vitality and growth just waiting to be released.

Such ignorance is by no means bliss!

Ignorance of spiritual gifts may be a chief cause of retarded church growth today. It also may be at the root of much of the discouragement, insecurity, frustration and guilt that plagues many Christian individuals and curtails their total effectiveness for God.

Are you really the Christian God wants you to be? If not, perhaps this book will help to head you in a different and more productive direction. Be assured that dispelling the fog of ignorance about spiritual gifts is no magic formula for instant spirituality. The relationship of each one of us to God is a tender and complex combination of factors which constantly need to be balanced one against another. However, other things being equal, you may soon come to experience a liberating, invigorating, and uplifting encounter with God's Holy Spirit as you discover the most basic step a Christian needs to take to define God's will for his or her life—knowing your spiritual gift or gifts.

To many this will sound so appealing that they will begin to doubt my credibility. They will wonder if I haven't overstated myself.

I do not think I have. I personally feel very strongly that what I have said is valid. The vitality that knowing about spiritual gifts contributes to the Christian life has been impressed on me from two sources. The first source is the Word of God. All Scripture has been inspired by God so that "the man of God may be . . . thoroughly furnished unto all good works" (2 Tim. 3:16,17). The first source for a sense of direction in finding ourselves spiritually, then, must be the Bible, and there is no substitute for it.

But the other source, while secondary, has been equally essential for my conclusion. It is my own experience. On a recent radio interview I was asked what was my most important spiritual experience other than my conversion. I did not hesitate in answering that it was discovering my spiritual gifts. As the book progresses, I will describe in some detail how this happened in my life, so there is no need to elaborate here.

Let's go directly to the primary source, then—the Word of God.

God's Way for Finding God's Will

One of the Scripture texts most frequently recommended to new Christians for memory is Romans 12:1 2. It certainly was among those I first memorized when I became a Christian 27 years ago, and I have never forgotten it. Here it is:

> *I beseech you therefore, brethren, by the mercies of God, that ye present your bodies a living sacrifice, holy, acceptable unto God, which is your reasonable service. And be not conformed to this world; but be ye transformed by the renewing of your mind, that ye may prove what is that good, and acceptable, and perfect, will of God.*

I think that the last phrase of this passage is the one which makes it so appealing to new Christians. Doing the "good, and acceptable, and perfect, will of God" is the sincere, heartfelt desire of every person who has been truly born again. When a person realizes that Jesus paid the ultimate price—His blood poured out on the cross—to save him or her, the first thing he or she says is, "Thank you, God. I love you for what you did. I want to serve you. Now tell me what you want me to do."

These two verses, however, pose a problem even to veteran Christians, to say nothing of new ones. To be honest, they are not very practical. By pure coincidence, last Sunday my own pastor, Raymond Ortlund, preached a sermon on this passage. Because I knew I was going to be writing on it this week, I listened with a great deal of attention. I was impressed with the combination of exegetical and homiletical energy he needed to exert in order to make the meaning clear to the congregation. The meaning of such concepts as "presenting bodies a living sacrifice" or "not being conformed to the world" or "being transformed by renewing the mind" is far from self-evident. They are wonderful verses, but rather abstract to say the least.

As I reflect back on my own spiritual pilgrimage I can recall that these verses did something for my life, but not very much. They felt good to recite for one thing. For another they gave me the general idea that part of living the kind of life that pleased God was to consecrate myself to Him. But where they let me down was in the practical area of finding God's will. I wanted to do the "good, and acceptable, and perfect, will of God," and all I could deduce from Romans 12:1,2 was that the more consecrated I became the more definitely I would then be able to know the will of God.

This idea, which I now call "consecration theology," was fairly widespread among the circle of Christian friends I was moving with. One of the major symbols of improved consecration was the Keswick campground in New Jersey. When critical decisions in life came up, we were frequently advised to spend a few days in Keswick. There, we were assured, we would come into the "deeper life," and through it God's will would become clear. As I look back I see that God, by His grace, did give me guidance through consecration theology. But even though you can go from Los Angeles to San Francisco on a bicycle or dig the foundation of a house with a teaspoon, there are better ways to do them.

A consecrated Christian life is necessary for doing God's will. No question about it. But in order to understand the really practical methodology for finding the "good, and acceptable, and perfect, will of God," you need to read forward to Romans 12:3-6, not backward to Romans 12:1,2. This is the better way. This is digging a foundation with a Caterpillar tractor rather than with a teaspoon.

Gift Theology

The key to coming to practical terms with the will of God for our lives is to "think soberly" of ourselves, according to verse 3. This means that each of us needs a realistic self-evaluation as a starting point. The *Phillips* translation says, "try to have a sane estimate of your capabilities."

Two steps need to be taken to arrive at this realistic self-evaluation, one negative and one positive.

Negatively, we are not allowed to think more highly of ourselves than we ought to think. In evaluating ourselves there is no room for pride. Sober judgments always involve humility. If one has to err, it is better to err on the side of being too humble rather than being too proud. But neither extreme is really necessary in light of the way God has arranged things for His children.

Positively, we are to recognize that part of our very spiritual constitution is a "measure of faith" which God has distributed to every Christian person. The implication is that every Christian may receive a different measure, and thereby every Christian is unique. But unique in what sense? Before Paul answers this question, he gives us the analogy he is preparing to use to explain spiritual gifts, the analogy of the human body.

From Romans 12:4 we learn that a very simple overview of our own physical body will give us what we might term a "hermeneutical key" to unlocking the biblical teaching on spiritual gifts. Hermeneutics is simply the theological word for biblical interpretation. So in order to comprehend the biblical teaching on spiritual gifts we need to keep a mental picture of our human body before us at all times.

This hermeneutical key is surprisingly uncomplicated. It does not involve knowledge of advanced anatomy or physiology or genetics. It simply requires the recognition that our one physical body is made up of many members and that each member of the one body has a different function. In other words if we understand that we cannot pick anything up with our ear and that we can't hear with our hand, we have the clue we need. Bodily members are designed to do their thing and no more. We err if we expect them to do what they are not designed to do.

So, with that, Paul goes on to say in Romans 12:5 that the Body of Christ operates exactly like the human body. Each Christian is a member of the Body of Christ, and as such has a particular function to perform just as the ear or the hand does. Furthermore, all are members of the same Body, so in some sense all Christians need each other.

That leads us to more questions. If I am a member of the Body, how do I know whether I am an ear or a hand or some other member? How do I know how I am supposed to function?

In answer, your purpose in the Body is determined by your spiritual gift or gift-mix. After Paul says we are members one of another, he adds, "having then *gifts* differing according to the grace that is given to us" (Rom. 12:6),[1] and then he begins a list of specific gifts.

My conclusion from this passage of Scripture, then, is that "gift theology" is probably more helpful for knowing God's will for your life in a practical way than is "consecration theology." To do the "good, and acceptable, and perfect, will of God" you must think soberly of yourself. To think soberly you must be realistic about your measure of faith. Your measure of faith is the spiritual gift that has determined which member of the Body you are and what is the special task God has given you to perform for the rest of your life.

How the Body of Christ Is Organized

What, precisely is the *Body of Christ* that we have been introduced to? Since the Bible says that we Christians are all one Body in Christ, we understand that it is a group of believers. In other biblical passages the Body is explicitly equated with the church. Ephesians 1, for example, talks about God setting Christ above all principalities and powers, putting all things under His feet, and giving Him "to be the head over all things to the *church, which is his body*" (Eph. 1:21-23). Colossians 1 says practically the same thing, namely that Jesus "is the head of *the body, the church*" (Col. 1:18). So, when I use *Body of Christ* in this book, I mean the same thing that the Bible means, namely the Christian church.

The church, of course, exists at many levels. It is the local fellowship of believers, it is the national denomination, it is the mission agency, and it is also the universal group of people from all countries of the world who acknowledge Christ as Lord and strive to serve Him. The *Body of Christ* refers to all of these. While I will use it for all, I will try to be specific enough in each context to indicate to which level I refer. At one or two points the realization that in one sense the Body of Christ refers to the universal church will become crucial to our understanding of certain aspects of spiritual gifts.

God Himself, of course, is the one who designed the Body of Christ. Therefore, before we ask the question as to how *we* should organize it, we need to ask how *He* organized it.

On one hand, God did not plan that the Body of Christ should be organized around the model of a dictatorship where just one person rules, benevolent as that person might be. But on the other hand, neither did He intend that it should be a democracy where every member rules. This latter point needs to be underlined here in America where our civil culture prides itself so much in democracy, and where this frequently is carried over into the churches.

As a Congregationalist I hate to admit it, but for growing churches the congregational form of government is like a millstone around its neck. It is reasonably functional for churches of one or two hundred members, but when churches grow to between 500 and 1,000 and up, they often will find their growth retarded unless the administrative system is streamlined. My own church, Lake Avenue Congregational, has now passed the 3,000 mark, but its growth through the years has been slow, due somewhat to the tenacious hold it maintains on congregational government. Making a decision in a large Congregational church reminds me of trying to turn the Queen Mary with an oar. It is incredibly difficult and highly frustrating at times.

Instead of a dictatorship or a democracy, God has chosen to make the Body of Christ an organism with Christ as the head and each member functioning with a spiritual gift. Understanding spiritual gifts, then, is the key to understanding the organization of the church.

Grace Community Church of the Valley in Panorama City, California is a church with an incredible growth rate of over 500 percent per decade and a current morning attendance of over 5,000. It is intentionally structured around the concept of spiritual gifts. Pastor John MacArthur says, "No local congregation will be what it should be, what Jesus prayed that it should be, what the Holy Spirit gifted it and empowered it to be, until it understands spiritual gifts."[2] John MacArthur is right, not only because he has proved that it works, but even more because he has captured the biblical concept of the organization of the Body.

The major biblical passages on spiritual gifts reinforce the above conclusion. It cannot be mere coincidence that in all three of the most explicit passages on spiritual gifts, Romans 12, 1 Corinthians 12, and Ephesians 4, the gifts are explained in the context of the Body. "God set the members, every one of them in the body, as it hath pleased him" (1 Cor. 12:18). This means that not only has God organized the Body on the model of an organism, but also that He has gone so far as to determine what the function of each of the members should be. Therefore, if you decide to organize your church around spiritual gifts, you are simply uncovering what God has already willed for your particular segment of Christ's Body.

Who Has Spiritual Gifts?

Not everybody has spiritual gifts. Unbelievers do not. But every Christian person who is committed to Jesus and truly a member of His Body has at least one gift, or possibly more. The Bible says that every Christian has received a gift (see 1 Pet. 4:10), and that "the manifestation of the Spirit is given to *every man* to profit" (1 Cor.

12:7). Even the verse we looked at in the last paragraph stresses that *every one* of the members is placed in the Body according to God's design (see 1 Cor. 12:18). No Christian whatsoever needs to feel left out when it comes to possessing a spiritual gift.

Many Christians are multi-gifted. How many are, I do not know. This is a fascinating subject waiting for further research. But I would suspect that probably the majority, or perhaps all Christians, have what we could call a "gift-mix" instead of a single gift. Given the variety of gifts, the degrees of giftedness in each case, and the multiple ministries through which each gift can be exercised, the combination of these qualities that I have been given and the combination that you have been given may be the most important factor in determining our spiritual personalities. We are used to the idea that each individual has his or her own personality. My wife and I have three daughters, all born of the same parents and raised in the same household, but they are each unique. God's children are probably similar. Every Christian is a unique member of the Body of Christ, and his or her identity is determined to a significant degree by the gift-mix he or she has been given.

The health of the church and its subsequent growth depend on this fact. Nazarene scholar, W.T. Purkiser, asserts that "every true function of the body of Christ has a 'member' to perform it, and every member has a function to perform."[3] I realize that it comes as a surprise to some Christians, who have been only marginally active in church for years, to find out that they are needed and wanted and gifted to do their part in the Body. But it is true. Unless there is some substitute for pleasing God, there is no substitute for finding your gift-mix and knowing for sure that you are doing just what God designed you to do.

I wish I didn't have to point this next thing out, but unfortunately I do. When Paul says that the Spirit has distributed the gifts to "every man to profit" (1 Cor. 12:7), he obviously means to every *person*. Women, as well as men, are members of the Body and receive spiritual gifts.

I felt badly some months ago when I saw an article by Nancy Hardesty in which she argued, with a good bit of verve, that women had spiritual gifts too. I felt badly, not because of the article itself, which was excellent, but because such an article had to be written at all. In it she laments that women have been assigned a disproportionately low profile by evangelical churches in general, and I believe this observation is accurate.

If just women, who constitute over 50 percent of the church membership in the United States, could be encouraged and allowed to use their spiritual gifts a tremendous dynamic for growth would be released that now is largely stifled. Not only that, but Nancy Hardesty points out something else that might be even more important. "Ultimately the refusal to allow women to fully use their gifts in the church and in the world is a form of blasphemy against the Holy Spirit."[4] These are strong words, but when you think it through theologically, she probably has a very good point.

God's Gifts and God's Call

It is common for Christians to speak of their "calling." Part of our religious vocabulary is that "God has called me to do such and such," or "I don't believe God is calling me to do such and such." It is helpful to recognize that a person's "call" and his or her spiritual gifts are very closely associated.

When related to the objective of doing God's will or functioning in the Body of Christ, a person's *general* call is equivalent to his or her spiritual gift. There is no better framework within which to interpret one's call than one's gift-mix. God does not give gifts which He does not "call" the recipient to use, nor does He call someone to do something for Him without equipping that person with the necessary gift or gifts to do it.

However, besides the *general* calling there will also be a *specific* calling. Some like to refer to this specific call as one's "ministry." So the ministry or the specific call determines the particular way or the particular setting in which God wishes you to exercise the gift or gifts He has given you. For example, a person can have the gift of teaching and be called specifically to use that gift among children or on the radio or in writing books. A person can have the missionary gift and be called to use that gift in Zambia. Within the general calling provided by each gift, then, are many more specific ways that such a gift can be ministered.

What Is a Spiritual Gift?

At this point we need to pause and define just what *spiritual gift* means. The working definition I like to use is as follows:

A spiritual gift is a special attribute given by the Holy Spirit to every member of the Body of Christ according to God's grace for use within the context of the Body.

This is as tight and economical a definition as I have been able to formulate and still retain what I consider to be the essential elements. Several of these elements, namely "special attribute," "given by the Spirit," and "to every member of the Body of Christ" have been sufficiently discussed. Two phrases remain.

"According to God's grace" is a phrase that moves into the biblical words themselves. The common Greek word for spiritual gift is *charisma*, with the plural *charis-*

mata. It is immediately obvious that our contemporary terms, "charismatic movement" or "charismatics" are derived from this Greek word. But there is something more to it, since *charisma* comes from the word *charis*, which in Greek means grace. There is a very close relationship, then, between spiritual gifts and the grace of God.

While a thorough biblical word study is not called for here, it might be helpful just to note in passing a couple of things concerning the Greek words.

First, *charismata* is not an exclusive synonym for spiritual gifts. It is used with other meanings in the Bible such as in Romans 6:23, "For the wages of sin is death; but the gift *[charisma]* of God is eternal life through Jesus Christ our Lord."

Secondly, *charismata* is not the only word used in the New Testament for spiritual gifts, although it is the most common one. For example, in 1 Corinthians 12:1, "Now, concerning spiritual gifts, brethren, . . . " the Greek word *pneumatikos*, more literally "spiritual things" or "spirituals," is used. However, as this is elaborated in the rest of the chapter *charismata* is used five times. Another word used for spiritual gifts in Ephesians 4:8 is *domata* (singular, *doma*), a more general Greek word for gifts. But even here in the context it is closely related to grace in the preceding verse: "Unto every one of us is given grace *[charis]* according to the measure of the gift of Christ" (Eph. 4:7). This phrase is reminiscent of the "measure of faith" of Romans 12:3 which also is tied in to *charismata* in Romans 12:6.

So much for the Greek. The major purpose in bringing this up was to indicate the intimate relationship that spiritual gifts have to the grace of God. This is why we include "according to God's grace" in the working definition.

The final phrase in the definition is "for use within the context of the Body." Individual Christians disconnected from the Body are not very useful. Spiritual gifts are not designed for Lone Rangers. They are designed for members of the Body. Professor Jack MacGorman of Southwestern Baptist Seminary puts it well when he says, "Not only are the gifts *functional*, but they are also *congregational*,"[5] Most of the things God does in the world are done through Christians who are working together in community, complementing each other with their gifts in their local congregations.

The context of the Body, as I use the term, does not mean that gifts are always inward-looking, for use just within the church and for the mutual benefit of Christians. Many gifts such as evangelist and missionary and service need to benefit those who are not yet members of the Body. But the point is that these gifts, even when moving outward from the Body, are still to be used not just by individuals but by Christians working as a team if the job is to be done in the best possible way.

Discover, Develop and Use Your Gift

If spiritual gifts at work are as important to God and to the church and to individual Christians as I have tried to describe, something better be done about them in a practical, personal way. In the light of the clear teaching of God's Word, I do not think I am amiss in stating that one of the primary spiritual exercises for any Christian person is to discover, develop and use his or her spiritual gift. Other spiritual exercises may be equally as important: worship, prayer, reading God's Word, feeding the hungry, or what have you. But I do not know of anything *more* important than discovering, developing and using spiritual gifts.

A Christian desiring to do the will of God, but who

does not know how he or she was made to function in the Body of Christ, needs to give top priority to discovering gifts. Elizabeth O'Connor, from the Church of the Savior in Washington, D.C., a church nationally known for the use of spiritual gifts, puts it this way: "We ask to know the will of God without guessing that his will is written into our very beings. We perceive that will when we discern our gifts."[6]

"Discover" comes before "develop" in the sequence because spiritual gifts are received, not achieved. God gives the gifts at His own discretion. First Corinthians 12:11 talks about the Spirit dividing gifts "to every man severally *as he will*." Later in verse 18 the text says that God sets the members in the Body *"as it hath pleased him."* God has not entrusted any person to give spiritual gifts. No pastor, no district superintendent, no seminary president, not even the Pope himself is qualified to dispense spiritual gifts.

Furthermore, no one works real hard and is then rewarded with a gift. They are gifts of grace and, as such, they emerge from God with no reference to the degree of merit or sanctification that the recipient may have attained. The fact that they are given to a brand new Christian even before he or she has had time to mature in the Body of Christ confirms this.

Is "Discovering Gifts" Counterproductive?

Gene Getz, professor at Dallas Seminary and founding pastor of the dynamic Fellowship Bible Church of Dallas, is one of America's outstanding Bible teachers and churchmen. Getz disagrees with the idea that it is important to Christians to discover their spiritual gifts. For many years he himself taught that Christians should make an effort to discover gifts, but more recently he has reversed his position.[7]

Getz' point of view deserves thoughtful consideration. For one thing he is a thorough Bible student and would not be inclined to draw such conclusions hastily. For another, and directly apropos to this book, the church he planted in 1972, Fellowship Bible Church, has enjoyed remarkable growth. In articulating the philosophy of ministry for his church Getz stresses the concept of "body maturity." He emphasizes faith, hope and love along with the leadership qualities listed in 1 Timothy 3 and Titus 1 instead of emphasizing spiritual gifts.

In his book, *Building Up One Another*, Getz lists the reasons he rejects the idea of discovering spiritual gifts. These reasons serve to catalog some of the real pitfalls you need to avoid, no matter which position you decide to take. It would be well to mention them here so that we can keep them in mind as we move along with the discussion. Let me summarize them:

1. *Confusion*. Teaching Christians to discover spiritual gifts they received at conversion has, in fact, caused many people, even mature believers, to become confused.
2. *Rationalization*. Some tend to fix their attention on a supposed gift and use it as a rationalization for not fulfilling other biblical responsibilities. For example, a person might say he or she has the gift of pastoring, but not of teaching. Or someone may say that he or she does not have the gift of evangelism because they feel uncomfortable sharing Christ.
3. *Self-deception*. Some people think they have a spiritual gift when they really don't.

Getz is strong on this teaching because, as he says, "it suddenly dawned on me one day" that nowhere in 1 Corinthians 12, Romans 12 or Ephesians 4 "can we find any exhortation for individual Christians to 'look for' or to 'try to discover' their spiritual gift or gifts."[8]

I have thought about Getz' position quite a bit. Questions about it often come up in my seminars. I hesitate to contradict him because, after all, he is a successful church planter and pastor. I have great personal admiration for fellow seminary professors who are able (I might say, "who have the appropriate mix of spiritual gifts") to combine the practical with the theoretical as well as Gene Getz does.

Nevertheless, I will say that I don't think Getz has given sufficient consideration to Romans 12:1-6. I do not have to go into detail since it has been discussed previously except to point out once again what seems to me to be a clear logical relationship between "having gifts" (see Rom. 12:6) and "thinking soberly of oneself" (see Rom. 12:3) and doing the "good, and acceptable, and perfect, will of God" (Rom. 12:2).

Now I will be the first to admit that there are many mature, faithful and useful Christian people who are doing God's will without being able to describe in clear terms what their specific gift is. Certainly many believers through the centuries, throughout the world, and specifically here in America, previous to the "new thing" I spoke about in the Introduction, have been doing God's will in outstanding ways. Many are in fact using their spiritual gifts without being able to articulate what they are doing. Nevertheless, I sincerely believe that such brethren are operating under God's "Plan B." I think that Romans 12:1-6 is clear enough to teach us that God's "Plan A" is for members of the Body of Christ to be very conscious of the part each one plays in the "whole body fitly joined together" (Eph. 4:16). "Plan B" is functional. But "Plan A" is probably God's best.

The fact that many churches, whose philosophy of

ministry is "Plan B," are growing only reaffirms what church growth leaders often state: church growth is complex. It is possible for a church to score low on one growth principle and still grow if other growth principles are operating effectively. A particular view on spiritual gifts is not some surefire formula for church growth. But in *many cases* (not all) an awakening to spiritual gifts, mobilizing the membership around the gifts as biblically identified and defined, and encouraging the Body to begin functioning with its members working together by the power of the Holy Spirit will help a church get out of the growth doldrums as surely as a vaccination will prevent smallpox.

The objections Gene Getz raises to the practical discovery and use of spiritual gifts are real. Confusion, rationalization, and self-deception can and do pose serious problems. But they are not insuperable obstacles. Confusion can be eliminated when strong biblical teaching on gifts is provided in a context of sensitive pastoral care. Rationalization is less useful as a cop-out when the proper relationship between gifts and roles is clarified. Self-deception evaporates when the Body functions well enough so that members share their perceptions of each others' gifts with openness and love.

Before closing the subject of discovering spiritual gifts, we need to look briefly at two sets of texts which have caused problems for some.

The first is a pair of related verses, 1 Corinthians 12:31 and 1 Corinthians 14:1. Both of them say to "covet" or "desire" spiritual gifts. But neither of these verses is addressed to individual Christians. Both refer to the church at Corinth as a whole, a church which had fallen into the particular error of elevating the gift of tongues above all other gifts. These verses need not be considered normative for us as individuals.

The second is another related pair, 1 Timothy 4:14 and 2 Timothy 1:6. In these verses Paul states that Timothy received a gift by the laying on of hands, Paul's hands and the hands of the presbytery. The common interpretation of this, in light of the many other Scriptures on the subject, is that the function of a presbytery is to lay on hands when the gift that God has given is recognized by the Body and this act authorizes ministry with the gift in an official way. Whatever function other believers might have in confirming gifts, it must be remembered that the Spirit distributes gifts "as he will" (1 Cor. 12:11).

The Benefits of Spiritual Gifts

What happens when you decide to discover, develop and use your spiritual gift or gifts?

First of all, you will be a better Christian and more able to allow God to make your life count for Him. People who know their gifts have a handle on their "spiritual job description," so to speak. They find their place in the church with more ease. I have often said, half in jest, that one immediate benefit of the people in a church knowing their spiritual gifts is that the nominating committee can be phased out and a screening committee set up to receive applications for work. Now I don't joke about it as much. A few months ago I received a letter from Pastor Paul Erickson of First Covenant Church of Portland, Oregon, who had been studying church growth in the Fuller Doctor of Ministry program. His letter said, "Our people have joined the exciting search for discovering and using their spiritual gifts. Six of our people contacted the nominating committee for service on the boards next year!"

Christian people who know their spiritual gifts tend to develop healthy self-esteem. This does not mean that they "think more highly of themselves than they ought to think." They learn that no matter what their gift is, they are important to God and to the Body. The ear learns not to say, "because I am not the eye, I am not of the body" (1 Cor. 12:16). Crippling inferiority complexes drop by the wayside when people begin to "think soberly of themselves."

Humility is a Christian virtue, but like most good things it can be overdone. Some Christians are so humble they are virtually useless to the Body. This is false humility, and it is often stimulated by ignorance of spiritual gifts.

People who refuse to name their spiritual gift on the grounds that they would be arrogant and presumptuous, only exhibit their ignorance of the biblical teaching on gifts. Some may even have a trickier motive for not wanting to be associated with a gift—they do not want to be held accountable for its use. In that case, humility is used as a cover-up for disobedience.

Most people who know their spiritual gifts are not bogged down by such negative attitudes. They love God, they love their brothers and sisters, they love themselves for what God has made them to be. They are not proud of their gifts but they are thankful for them. They work together with other members of the Body in harmony and effectiveness.

Secondly, not only does knowing about spiritual gifts help individual Christians, but it helps the church as a whole. Ephesians 4 tells us that when spiritual gifts are in operation, the whole Body matures. It helps the Body to become "a perfect man" and "no more children" (Eph. 4:13,14).

When the church matures, predictably it grows. When the Body is functioning well and "each separate part works as it should, the whole body grows" (Eph.

4:16, *TEV*). There is clearly a biblical relationship between spiritual gifts and church growth. This whole book is an elaboration of how this relationship works out in practice.

The third and most important thing that knowing about spiritual gifts does is that it glorifies God. First Peter 4:10,11 advises Christians to use their spiritual gifts, then adds the reason why: "That God in all things may be glorified through Jesus Christ, to whom be praise and dominion for ever and ever. Amen." What could be better than glorifying God? It is the "chief end of man," according to the Westminster Catechism.

Stewardship of Gifts: Dangers and Delights

The Bible tells us clearly and directly that Christians are stewards of their spiritual gifts (see 1 Pet. 4:10).

Stewardship, in the New Testament sense, is an awesome responsibility. Awesome, because the very notion of stewardship carries with it an important dimension of accountability.

According to 1 Corinthians 4:2, "It is required in stewards, that a man be found faithful." This verse has often been misinterpreted. I have heard people quote it and follow with the statement, "God doesn't require success, He just requires faithfulness." This kind of conclusion can become a pious excuse for a Christian person's laziness, blundering, incompetence, or lack of courage. By no means is that what New Testament stewardship implies.

The key to stewardship is found in the parable of the talents in Matthew 25:14-30. Three stewards in the business world received different quantities of capital. Their responsibility was to use that resource for its purpose in the business world—to make more money. Two of the three doubled their money and when the day of accounting came, they were called "good and *faithful* servants." Faithfulness was directly related to success. The other steward was timid and a negative thinker. He could not recognize the potential of the resource he had. He did nothing with his capital, and thus was judged a "wicked and slothful servant."

Every spiritual gift we have is a resource that we must use and for which we will be held accountable at the judgment. Some will have one, some two, and some five. The quantity to begin with does not matter. Stewards are responsible only for what the master has chosen to give them. But the resource that we do have *must* be used to accomplish the master's purpose. There is no time like now to begin to prepare to answer that question which each of us eventually is going to hear from our Lord: "What did you do with the spiritual gift I gave you?"

Tragically, many will not be able to answer that question. They will not be called "good and faithful servants," at least in that area of their lives, because they have been ignorant of spiritual gifts. Ignorance is not bliss!

Gifts Can Be Abused

There are many ways that spiritual gifts can be abused. United Methodist scholar Kenneth Kinghorn describes the extremes with the colorful words *charisphobia* and *charismania*.[9] Some who are fully aware of the potential of spiritual gifts use them for acquiring power or gaining wealth or taking revenge or exploiting fellow believers. I will not attempt to expand on these or catalog all other abuses of spiritual gifts common today. But I do want to name and comment on two of them which I consider to be especially widespread and counterproductive for church growth.

The first is gift exaltation. In some circles it is popular to exalt one gift over the others. Having a certain gift constitutes a spiritual status symbol in some groups. The first class citizens are separated from the second class citizens on the basis of exercising a certain gift or gifts.

When this happens, gifts tend to become ends in themselves. They glorify the user rather than the giver. They benefit the individual rather than the Body. They produce pride and self-indulgence. The Corinthians had fallen into this trap, and Paul writes 1 Corinthians 12–14 in an attempt to straighten them out. All of us need to take fair warning and avoid gift exaltation.

As I reviewed the literature on spiritual gifts, I found gift exaltation cropping up in unexpected places. One author, for example, calls prophecy the greatest gift. Another says it is the word of wisdom. Yet another suggests it might be apostleship. I myself do not believe that any one gift is above all others. It seems that certain ones may be more appropriate than others for certain occasions, for certain places, for certain philosophies of ministry, for certain groups and for certain tasks. In the Corinthian situation, prophecy was needed more than tongues, for example. As Charles Hummel says, "Paul consistently selects and orders gifts randomly in order to illustrate diversity, rather than to indicate rank. Where there appears to be a logical order, it must be understood in the context of the passage and not made an absolute for all occasions."[10]

The second abuse is gift projection. Most Christians who have biographies written about them have accomplished extraordinary things during their lifetimes. What gave them the ability to turn in the kind of lifetime performance that would justify a biography? It has to be that God had given them a spiritual gift or gifts in an unusual degree, that they developed them diligently, and that they used them to the glory of God and for the benefit of the Body of Christ.

Few biographers, however, and few heroes of the biography have been people sensitive to the biblical teaching on spiritual gifts. This has caused them to take another approach toward explaining the cause of their unusual feats. Ordinarily the approach tends toward "consecration theology" rather than "gift theology." In other words the idea comes across that so-and-so did what he or she did simply because they loved God so much. Ergo, if you loved God that much, dear reader, you could do the same thing. If you are not able to do these things, you now know the reason why. There is something deficient in your relationship to God.

Many Christians who read these biographies, as a matter of fact, are consecrated to God. Because of this they are often the ones who feel the most frustrated, guilty and defeated when they learn about these giants of the faith. To make matters worse, when the heroes of the biographies are ignorant of spiritual gifts, they engage in what I call "gift projection." They tend to say, in honest humility, "Look, I'm just an ordinary Christian, no different from anyone else. Here's what I do, and God blesses it. If you just do what I do, God will bless you in the same way." What they don't say, unfortunately is, "I can do what I do because God has given me a certain gift or gift-mix. If you discover that God has given you the same, join me in this. If not, we will love and help each other as different members of the Body."

People in the syndrome of gift projection want the whole Body to be an eye. They unwittingly impose guilt and shame on fellow Christians. They make feet say, "Because I am not the hand, I am not of the body" (1 Cor. 12:15). They usually have no idea how devastating gift projection is for less gifted members of the Body. They are like the steward in the parable who came back with ten talents saying to the one who came back with four. "If you loved the master more, you would have come back with ten also," without mentioning that the master gave him five to start with but gave the other only two.

People who employ gift projection, and this is by no means confined to the deceased, not only impose a guilt trip on others, but more seriously they fail to recognize that the reason others are different from them and may have two talents instead of five is that the Holy Spirit Himself has divided "to every man severally as *he will*" (1 Cor. 12:11). In a way they are calling into question the wisdom and sovereignty of God at that point. They are indulging in the "creator complex"—intent on making others over in their own image.

George Muller of Bristol, England, for example, has been called the "apostle of faith." A number of biographies have been written about him describing the way God worked through him to care for orphans about a hundred years ago. I have read some of them and have got to say that George Muller would be listed in the *Guinness Book of Spiritual World Records*, if such a book were published then. He had other gifts as well, but one of his greatest was the gift of faith. Muller, however, as far as I know, never recognized this as a spiritual gift. At a high point in the biography, when readers are appropriately dazzled by his spiritual feats, Mr. Muller says, "Let not Satan deceive you in making you think you could not have the same faith, but that it is only for persons situated as I am . . . I pray to the Lord and expect an answer to my requests; and may not you do the same, dear believing reader?"[11]

At one point, earlier in my Christian life, I used to

read quite a few biographies. Then I stopped almost completely and at first did not know the reason why. What I did know is that, while they were enjoyable reading, when I finished I felt miserable. I always felt that "if he can do it so should I." Now I guess I know why I stopped reading them—I didn't like feeling miserable! The "dear believing reader" bit got to me. I was an unsuspecting victim of gift projection and because I was still operating out of the assumptions of consecration theology rather than gift theology, I did not know quite what to do about it.

In the chapters that follow, as we deal with specific gifts, I will refer back from time to time to the syndrome of gift projection. Not only do I have the personal feelings about it already described, but I also believe that in many cases it is hindering the growth of churches.

And it is time now to get specific on the 27 individual gifts.

Notes

1. Hereafter italics in quoted Scripture passages are added by the author for emphasis.
2. John MacArthur, Jr., *The Church—the Body of Christ* (Grand Rapids: Zondervan Publishing House, 1973), p. 136.
3. W.T. Purkiser, *The Gifts of the Spirit* (Kansas City: Beacon Hill Press, 1975), p. 21.
4. Nancy Hardesty, "Gifts," *The Other Side* (July-August, 1977), p. 40.
5. Jack W. MacGorman, *The Gifts of the Spirit* (Nashville, Broadman Press, 1974), p. 31.
6. Elizabeth O'Connor, *Eighth Day of Creation: Gifts and Creativity* (Waco, Word Books, 1971), p. 15.
7. Gene A. Getz develops this point in two of his works. The earlier is *Sharpening the Focus of the Church* (Chicago: Moody Press, 1974), pp. 112-117; and more recently in *Building Up One Another* (Wheaton: Victor Books, 1976), pp. 9-16.
8. Getz, *Building Up One Another*, p. 9.
9. Kenneth Cain Kinghorn, *Gifts of the Spirit* (Nashville: Abingdon Press, 1976), p. 95.
10. Charles E. Hummel, *Fire in the Fireplace* (Downers Grove, Inter-Varsity Press, 1978), p. 246.
11. Basil Miller, *George Muller: The Man of Faith* (Grand Rapids. Zondervan Publishing House, 1941), p. 58.

2.
What the Gifts Are: An Open-Ended Approach

Before we can discuss any more of the implications of spiritual gifts for church growth, we need to be as specific as we can about what the gifts really are and which ones are available for churches today.

The approach to this is going to be as open-ended as possible. Since, as we will see in some detail, the Bible does not lock us into tight restrictions as to the number of gifts, this seems to be a legitimate procedure. My intention is to do this in such a way that any church that wants to use spiritual gifts to help it grow will be able to fit in.

I think this can be done because I believe so strongly in the universality of spiritual gifts. Every Christian has them and every church has them. Many are still buried in the ground like the talent in Matthew 25, but they can be unearthed and used for the glory of God and the growth of the church. Spiritual gifts are for Methodist churches and Conservative Baptist churches. They are for Holiness churches and Pentecostal churches. They are for Arminian churches and Calvinistic churches. They are for small churches and large churches, suburban churches and inner city churches, black churches and white churches. They are for churches that use the *Scofield Bible* and churches that use the *Revised Standard Version*. They are for every church of which Christ is the head and the members are parts of His Body.

And spiritual gifts work. When they don't, there is something wrong with the Body's health. If the Bible is clear about anything, it is clear that God (1) wants every Christian to have and use a spiritual gift or gifts, and (2) He wants His lost sheep to be found and His church to grow. Spiritual gifts are utilitarian. They are functional. They have a task to do and if they are working properly, the task will be accomplished. When the gifts work together in a church that wants to grow and is willing to pay the price for growth, the church will see God's blessing and will grow.

As the book progresses, I am going to describe 27 different spiritual gifts. This is no magic number. There are probably more, there may even be fewer. This variation will be explained in due time.

The order in which the gifts are described needs to be pointed out. Some books take them in the order in which they appear in the Bible. Some describe them as subpoints under several major classifications. At least one deals with them in alphabetical order. I have decided on a procedure somewhat different from the others in that it is more of a functional order. The gifts will be discussed as they naturally come up and need to be emphasized for their particular function in the growth of the church. In this chapter, for example, I will mention all 27 gifts, but discuss only four. In the next chapter I will discuss four more, and so on. A special table in the front of the book on page 9 will indicate where each gift comes up for its principal discussion. Other places where a gift is mentioned can be located in the index.

The Three Key Lists

The great majority of the spiritual gifts mentioned in the Bible are found in three key chapters: Romans 12; 1 Corinthians 12; and Ephesians 4. It is well to memorize these three locations for future reference because they are primary. There are also several secondary chapters that fill us in on other important details. They include mainly 1 Corinthians 13—14; 1 Peter 4; 1 Corinthians 7 and Ephesians 3.

We will begin putting the master list together by using the three primary chapters. The words in parentheses are variant translations of the same Greek word.

Romans 12 mentions the following spiritual gifts:

1. Prophecy (preaching, inspired utterance)
2. Service (ministry)
3. Teaching
4. Exhortation (stimulating faith, encouraging)
5. Giving (contributing, generosity, sharing)
6. Leadership (authority, ruling, administration)
7. Mercy (sympathy, comfort to the sorrowing, showing kindness)

First Corinthians 12 adds (without repeating those already listed from Romans):

8. Wisdom (wise advice, wise speech)
9. Knowledge (studying, speaking with knowledge)
10. Faith
11. Healing

12. Miracles (doing great deeds)
13. Discerning of spirits (discrimination in spiritual matters)
14. Tongues (speaking in languages never learned, ecstatic utterance)
15. Interpretation of tongues
16. Apostle
17. Helps
18. Administration (governments, getting others to work together)

Ephesians 4 adds (again, without repeating any of the above):

19. Evangelist
20. Pastor (caring for God's people)

Church Offices and the Peter Principle

Some may point out that the list in Ephesians 4 is slightly different from the other two in that it mentions offices rather than gifts as such. This is correct. When it speaks of apostles, prophets, evangelists and pastor-teachers being given to the church (see Eph. 4:11) the focus is placed on individuals who have been recognized in such official positions in the church. Usually such people have been ordained with a public laying on of hands. In modern day language they would probably be considered as "clergy" or part of the church or denominational staff.

Among Christian churches today there is a considerable variation as to which offices are recognized. Some feel that Ephesians 4:11 locks them into a certain number, some take a cue from the Pastoral Epistles that mention elders and deacons and bishops, and some go beyond this. African Independent churches, for example, have many officially-recognized apostles and prophets, whereas Nazarenes have neither of these. But

Nazarenes have offices of evangelist and general superintendent and district superintendent. The Southern Baptists call their district superintendents executive secretaries of state conventions; the Church of God (Cleveland) calls them state overseers; and the Seventh-Day Adventists call them conference presidents. People in charge of local churches are variously called pastors or ministers or priests. The Salvation Army has proper officers: lieutenants and captains and generals. And we could go on.

For some this may be confusing. For others, it is one more indication of the flexibility, the creativity, and the rich variety inherent in the very fiber of the Christian faith.

But the main purpose of bringing it up here is to point out that no matter what the office is named, the person who is called or ordained or commissioned to fill that office should qualify for it on the basis of the particular spiritual gift-mix that God has given to him or her. The apostle ought to have the gift of apostle, the prophet the gift of prophecy, and so forth.

Herein lies a frequent growth problem in American churches. People are allowed to occupy ecclesiastical offices with little or no reference to whether they have the appropriate spiritual gifts. Offices are often awarded on the basis of seniority, influence, personality, political manipulation, prestige, rotation or all of the above. I am afraid that the "Peter Principle" is more rampant in our churches than it ought to be. For the uninitiated, the Peter Principle was first articulated by best-selling author Lawrence Peter. His principle is that "In a hierarchy every employee tends to rise to his level of incompetence."[1] The final promotion for any individual is predictably from a level of competence to a level of incompetence, and there he stops. Most of Peter's illustrations come from business, government and industry, but he could as easily have illustrated the principle from the church.

Lawrence Peter laments the fact that in government and industry the principle is almost inexorable and, alas, our society is doomed to incompetence and mediocrity. But this need not and ought not to be the state of affairs in the church. God did not design the church for mediocrity. He knew about the Peter Principle before Lawrence Peter was born, and He designed a system to avoid it. If we filled our church offices on the basis of recognized spiritual gifts we would not be victimized by the Peter Principle. And we would unlock tremendous potential for growth that is now dormant and wasting away.

Completing the Master List

The three primary lists give us 20 separate gifts. Counting the words used for them in other versions, there could be more than double that number, but at this point we are going to stay with the 20.

One thing becomes immediately evident from the three primary lists—none of the lists is complete in itself. There are gifts mentioned in Ephesians that are also mentioned in Romans, and some in Romans mentioned in 1 Corinthians, and some in 1 Corinthians mentioned in Ephesians. Apparently, they are not intended to be complete catalogs of gifts that God gives. And one could surmise that if none of the three lists is complete in itself, probably the three lists together are not complete.

The Bible itself confirms that this is a correct assumption. There are at least five other gifts mentioned in the New Testament as such. They include:

21. Celibacy (continence)
22. Voluntary poverty

23. Martyrdom
24. Hospitality
25. Missionary

I am going to postpone discussing voluntary poverty and the missionary gift because they come up more naturally in other contexts. But at this point I do want to take a closer look at the other three because they will teach us some valuable lessons needed just at this point.

Gift 21: The Gift of Celibacy

Some adult Christians are married, some are single. Obviously, more are married than are single, and this is the way God intended it to be. Many single Christian adults (not all, however) are that way because God has given them the special gift of celibacy. God has so constituted them that by remaining single they can better accomplish His will for their lives.

The gift of celibacy is the special ability that God gives to some members of the Body of Christ to remain single and enjoy it; to be unmarried and not suffer undue sexual temptations.

If you are single and know down in your heart that you would get married in an instant if a reasonable opportunity presented itself, you probably don't have the gift. If you are single and find yourself terribly frustrated by unfulfilled sexual impulses, you probably don't have the gift. But if neither of these things seems to bother you, rejoice—you may have found one of your spiritual gifts.

The biblical text for this is found in 1 Corinthians 7:7. There Paul discusses his own state of celibacy and calls it a *charisma*, a spiritual gift. Men and women who are celibate are part of God's plan for His people, and they should be accepted and honored as such.

Notice that no special gift is necessary to get married,

have sexual relations, and raise a family. God has made humans with organs and glands and passions so that the majority of people, Christians included, need to get married and they do just that.

This brings up an important general principle relating to spiritual gifts: there are more members of the Body of Christ who do not share a particular spiritual gift than there are those who do. More Christians do not have the gift of celibacy than have it. Likewise more Christians do not have the gift of pastor than have it. The same applies to prophecy and evangelism and teacher and leadership, and probably every other gift on the list.

The analogy of the physical body that Paul firmly established in Romans 12:4 as the model through which we are to understand spiritual gifts clarifies this. We know that in our own bodies the majority of members are not hands. More members are not eyes or kidneys or toes or teeth or elbows than are. God has determined that we have two eyes, and this is just enough to do the job of seeing on behalf of the hundreds of other members of the same body. The Bible says specifically that the whole body should not be an eye, because if it were, it couldn't hear or smell (see 1 Cor. 12:17).

The same applies to the Body of Christ. The Shakers made the mistake of universalizing the gift of celibacy, and now have all but died a natural death as a denomination. Not only did they cut off biological growth, but transfer and conversion growth became very remote possibilities for them. Their life-style could not appeal to very many people mainly because God has not made very many people that way. The Catholic Church also has perpetuated an unbiblical application of gifts by requiring all clergy to remain single whether they have the gift of celibacy or not.

It is reasonable to conclude that something less than

50 percent of the Body should be expected to have any particular gift. My hunch is that most of the percentages will come out far less than 50 percent. I have done some research on the gift of evangelist and found that the figure is more like 10 percent. Much more research needs to be done to discover what segment of the Body has the other gifts so that we can better understand the profile of a healthy, spiritual congregation.

Men and women with the gift of celibacy have tremendous advantages. Paul emphasizes these in 1 Corinthians 7. There he mentions, for example, that Christians with the gift of celibacy can actually serve the Lord better than those without it because they don't have to worry about how to please their husband or wife or family (see 1 Cor. 7:32-34). I have found this true in my own experience. It has become more vivid since I have developed a personal friendship with John Stott, one of today's most respected Bible teachers, authors, and Christian statesmen. John Stott and I are both members of the executive committee of the Lausanne Committee for World Evangelization, so we meet frequently in various parts of the world, enjoy fellowship with each other, and share many areas of mutual interest.

John Stott has the gift of celibacy, and because this is of special interest to me, I have observed the advantages he has over those who, like myself, do not. For one thing, I make it a habit to call home frequently when I am traveling. When I do, I usually talk to both daughters who still live at home and then to my wife, Doris. If I spend too much time traveling, I hear about it in kindly, but firm, ways. When I am home I give high priority to setting aside time to spend with my family. I plan dinner at home, Saturdays working around the house and yard with them, days out for sporting events and other entertainment, and longer camping vacations in the summer.

While I am busy doing this, John Stott is writing another book or planning another conference or preparing another lecture, or traveling to another country. No wonder I can't come near to keeping up with his output. He has written so many books that some Christian bookstores now feature a special John Stott rack!

Do I envy John Stott? Not in the least. If I did, I would be untrue to what the Bible teaches about spiritual gifts. I can't thank God enough for the contribution John is making to building up Christians and to the task of world evangelization. And myself? I wouldn't trade my wife and family for a hundred special Peter Wagner racks in Christian bookstores! In fact, because I do not have the gift of celibacy, without my wife and what she contributes to every area of my being, the work I attempt to do for the Lord would be a disaster.

The temptation of gift projection, described in chapter 1, is not frequent among those with the gift of celibacy. In fact, the celibate that I am aware of who has come closest to it is the apostle Paul himself. In 1 Corinthians 7 he gets so enthusiastic about the advantages he finds in being single (the chances are he was a widower at the time, according to many biblical scholars) that he says, "I would that all men were even as myself" (1 Cor. 7:7). But then, under the Spirit's inspiration, he catches himself and quickly says that he knows it really is a spiritual gift.

One more aspect of the gift of celibacy needs to be noted. Celibacy is one of the two gifts that cannot stand alone. (The other is missionary, which will be explained later on.) In other words, there is no merit whatsoever in being unmarried if that is all there is to it. Being unmarried should allow a man or woman to be more effective in the use of whatever other gift or gift-mix God gives to an individual. It must always be understood and used in the light of what else it will help the person to accomplish in the Body of Christ.

Gift 23: The Gift of Martyrdom

While 1 Corinthians 13 is known mostly as a chapter on love, it also has two lists of spiritual gifts (see 1 Cor. 13:1-3,8). Most of them are picked up from chapter 12, but two—voluntary poverty and martyrdom—are additions to the list. Martyrdom is expressed in the words: "though I give my body to be burned" (1 Cor. 13:3).

What is the gift of martyrdom? Once in a while I say in jest that it is the gift you use only once! But really it is broader than just dying for the faith. It is an attitude toward suffering and death that is quite unusual. The inbuilt law of human self-preservation is characteristic of most people, Christians and non-Christians. The average Christian does not welcome thoughts of persecution, suffering, torture or being murdered. Most will take it if it comes, but they certainly would not welcome it and they would make every effort to avoid it if possible.

The gift of martyrdom is a special ability that God has given to certain members of the Body of Christ to undergo suffering for the faith even to death while consistently displaying a joyous and victorious attitude that brings glory to God.

When death is imminent, but possibilities exist for escape, the person with the gift of martyrdom may well choose to suffer and die. Christians who have other gifts and feel that God wants them to continue to use them, but do not have the gift of martyrdom, will usually choose to flee.

This exact situation presented itself recently to my dear friend, Festo Kivengere, a colleague on the Lausanne Committee for World Evangelization. During Idi

Amin's reign of terror in Uganda, Festo Kivengere was a prominent and influential bishop of an Anglican diocese. In 1977 he raised his voice in protest when Amin had his beloved friend and archbishop, Janani Luwum, murdered. As a result Kivengere ended up on Amin's hit list. He and his wife decided they did not have the gift of martyrdom and fled for their lives. The hair-raising tale of escape is told in Bishop Kivengere's excellent book, *I Love Idi Amin.* [2] They are now here in America, and the unusual gifts of exhortation and evangelism that God has given to Festo Kivengere have been preserved for the blessing of the Body of Christ and the cause of world evangelization.

It is only recently that I have come fully to appreciate the gift of martyrdom. When my wife, Doris, and I first went to Bolivia as missionaries in 1956, we were stationed in the tiny Chiquitano Indian village of Santiago de Chiquitos. It was from there that, 13 years previously, five New Tribes missionaries headed off into the jungle to contact the Ayore Indians and were never seen again.

George Haight, our senior missionary, knew the area and the people as few others. He said to the New Tribes missionaries, "If you do not take guns, you will not come back alive." They replied that they would prefer death to the glory of God rather than carry firearms. This was not a spur of the moment decision. I made a point to study their lives, their letters and their magazine articles because I was writing a book on the Ayores several years after the Ayores were contacted and were being evangelized. At first I came to the hasty and immature conclusion that the five suffered from a "martyr complex." I now see that both they and their wives were beautifully exercising a spiritual gift. The book that tells their story, written by one of the widows, expresses well the attitude of people with the gift of martyrdom: *God Planted Five Seeds.*[3]

In contrast, George Haight did not have the gift. His policy was to carry guns at all times and use them if necessary. On one of the unsuccessful expeditions to search for the five, the Ayores engaged Haight and his party in a jungle battle, and Haight shot and killed an Indian brave in self-defense.[4] He told me later that he felt that in the total economy of God, his life would count more over the next 20 years than that of the Ayore. God has blessed him, and he and his wife, Helen, were dearly loved by the people of the area for the selfless exercise of their gifts of service, helps, administration and missionary. He died of natural causes in 1978.

Stephen, of the church at Jerusalem, died a martyr's death. We do not have enough evidence to know if he had the gift of martyrdom, although his last words, "Lord, lay not this sin to their charge" (Acts 7:60), may carry a hint that he did. But we do know that his death resulted in tremendously accelerated church growth through Judea, Samaria, and even to the Gentiles in Antioch.

One of the murderers of the five New Tribes missionaries later found Christ and became an officer in the Ayore church. The well-known motto, "The blood of the martyrs is the seed of the church," expresses the relationship that this spiritual gift can have to church growth.

Gift 24: The Gift of Hospitality

The biblical text for the gift of hospitality is somewhat imprecise. First Peter 4:9 says, "Use hospitality ... without grudging," and then 1 Peter 4:10 immediately speaks of spiritual gifts. One legitimate way of interpreting the juxtaposition of the two verses is to understand that the use of hospitality is mentioned in verse 9, then attached to verse 10 with a "just as" word, so that it comes out paraphrased, "Use hospitality, just as all Christians have received any other spiritual gift."

If this seems to be stretching it, later on I suggest that hospitality should be listed as a spiritual gift whether or not it was mentioned in the Bible. I will give other illustrations of this principle shortly. But hospitality means "love of strangers," and some people undoubtedly have a special ability to do this for the glory of God and the growth of the church. I like to paraphrase Leslie Flynn's definition:

The gift of hospitality is that special ability that God gives to certain members of the Body of Christ to provide open house and warm welcome for those in need of food and lodging.[5]

Not only do those with the gift have the ability but they love to do it. Although it seems incredible to those of us who do not have the gift, people with the gift of hospitality are happier with guests in the home than they are alone. This is a supernatural ability given to only a few. Most people who don't have the gift find it a drag and a nuisance to have outsiders around their house for anything but short and well-monitored visits.

One person who has discovered that she has the gift of hospitality is Karen Mains, whose husband, David Mains, is well known for seminars on church renewal and for his book, *Full Circle.*[6] Karen Mains has written a whole book about hospitality, *Open Heart, Open Home.*[7] In an article on the subject in *Moody Monthly*, she says, "True hospitality is a gift of the Spirit," and explains that she received supernatural help for "creating heart-to-heart human bonds."[8] The motto of a person with this gift is "hospitality before pride," and one can often recognize its outworking when they enter such a home.

When guests are invited in, people without the gift want everything to be in place, rugs clean, furniture dusted, toys and newspapers picked up, fresh-cut flowers on the tables, candlelight, and the food something special, prepared and served just right. That's the way it invariably is when Doris and I have guests over, for example. To be honest, we do enjoy a neat, well-appointed home and want our guests to see it the way we believe it should be at its best. Maybe this is a sort of "pride before hospitality."

But people with the gift don't look at it like we do. Karen Mains tells how she is able to welcome a woman into her "unsightly rooms" and she refuses to embarrass her guest with apologies. She finds it uplifting, and describes it well in books and articles.

Those of us in the Body who don't have the gift, certainly are thankful for those who do. As missionaries on furlough, my family and I were frequently in the homes of fellow Christians who had the gift of hospitality. With a little experience, we could tell immediately whether the hosts had the gift. One of the outstanding couples who frequently cared for us were Glen and Irene Main of Bell, California. Whenever we were in their house we felt at home. Because they had the gift of hospitality, and because those with the gift always have the comfort of the visitor as their highest priority, the Mains on one occasion went out and purchased a car when they knew I was coming home for a time. They gave me the keys when I got off the plane. They began using it themselves only after I left again for Bolivia. We have many other friends, just as close to us and just as consecrated Christians and just as supportive of missionaries, who would never think of doing such a thing, nor would they be expected to. They have other gifts which Glen and Irene Main don't have. The Body needs them all.

Because the gift of hospitality is such a beautiful gift and so sincerely admired, those who have it need to be careful to avoid gift projection. I once visited L'Abri in Switzerland where Francis and Edith Schaeffer have a wonderful center for the spiritual renewal of troubled Christian young people. An atmosphere of hospitality oozes from every nook and cranny. When I arrived I immediately sensed that one of the two, if not both, must have the gift of hospitality.

Then I later read an article by Edith Schaeffer in *Christianity Today* in which she described her attitude toward hospitality.[9] Unfortunately, the article did not indicate that she recognizes she has special help from God to do what she is doing. The article's title, "Hospitality: Optional Or Commanded?" set the tone. As I read along I felt that she might have been indulging in gift projection, suggesting that other Christians who do not show L'Abri kind of hospitality may be something short of "doers of the Word, and not hearers only," as she states. If I didn't know about spiritual gifts I might have felt guilty about it.

The growth of the church in the Roman Empire in New Testament times was heavily dependent upon hospitality.[10] The exercise of hospitality was a cultural institution, essential for those who traveled as did the Christian missionaries. It was far different from travel conditions today with motels, hotels, Hertz cars and American Express cards. In fact when I travel for seminars, I request a single room in a hotel. All that is involved in staying in someone's home is an excessive drain on my energies and unnecessary in our American culture. When I travel abroad, however, it is a different story. Many cultures in the Third World are closer to that of the first century Roman Empire than ours in America, and hospitality there is more essential to the growth of the church. If we studied it, I think we would find a higher percentage of Christians in these circumstances are given the gift of hospitality. And even those without the gift have a higher expectation placed on them for entertaining guests than we expect in our more mechanized and individualized culture. In the first century, bishops and widows in particular had to be good at hospitality (see 1 Tim. 3:2; 1 Tim. 5:10).

Hospitality is very useful in church growth in America today when (1) evangelistic outreach is geared around evangelistic Bible studies that meet in homes, and (2) the church's philosophy of ministry includes multiplying house churches, as several successful, growing churches in America are demonstrating. More will be said about this later.

Are All Gifts Mentioned in the Bible?

Because none of the three primary lists is complete, and the three lists together are not complete, it is reasonable to conclude that the list of all the gifts mentioned in the Bible, and we have counted 25 of them, may not be complete either. If I may take the liberty, then, I am going to add two other gifts:

26. Intercession
27. Exorcism

This is what I mean by an open-ended approach to the gifts. I do not doubt that there are even more than 27 of them. Some might want to add the gift of music and make it 28 or craftsmanship and make it 29. I ran into another gift recently which might be called the "gift of names." Jerry Falwell, pastor of the renowned Thomas Road Baptist Church in Lynchburg, Virginia, is extraordinary in many ways. But one of them is that he knows the names of most of his 16,000 members! In fact, he can speak in another city, meet people afterwards, go back a year later, and remember the majority of the people he met by name. He himself says, "I have to give God credit for this . . . .It's a gift from God."[11] I'm so glad. I struggle for the 10 weeks of an academic quarter trying to attach names to the faces in my class; sometimes I succeed; and then one quarter later I pass a student on campus and say to myself, "What in the world is his name?" If I thought that God was going to hold me responsible for this in the final judgment, I think I would have a heart attack from excessive stress.

Because exorcism is closely related to the gift of discernment of spirits, I will discuss them together in another context. But we need to take a brief look at the gift of intercession now.

Gift 26: The Gift of Intercession

I have postulated the existence of this gift because I believe I have seen it in action.

Certain Christians, it seems to me, have a special ability to pray for extended periods of time on a regular basis and see frequent and specific answers to their prayers, to a degree much greater than that which is expected of the average Christian. This is the gift of intercession.

Since not too many other authors on spiritual gifts refer to it, I was glad when I read that Elizabeth O'Connor describes it at work in the Church of the Savior in Washington, D.C. She tells of a lady who came into one of the groups of their church and whom "the group had no difficulty in confirming as an intercessor. Confirmation of her gift did not mean that the rest of us would give up our prayers of intercession for each other and the group and its mission, but it did mean that we now had a person who would spend more time at the work of intercession."[12]

Because intercession is not widely accepted as a gift, many Christians tend not to recognize it when it comes. If prayer is as important as we all think it is, I find it curious that churches do not hire staff members to give themselves to intercession—staff is hired for just about everything else. Seminaries also ought to offer courses in prayer. I was pleasantly surprised recently when my friend, Robert Coleman, told me that Asbury Seminary has hired a Professor of Prayer, and has students who are majoring in prayer. Campus Crusade for Christ believes strongly in prayer, strongly enough to assign the responsibility to the president's wife, Vonette Bright. They have eight full-time staff members in their Prayer-Care ministry who go to work at the prayer chapel in Arrowhead Springs, California, pray for eight hours, and call it another day's work.[13]

How much time each day does a person with the gift of intercession spend in prayer? Perhaps eight hours. Perhaps only four; such as Mrs. Bernice Watne of Eagle Grove, Iowa. Mrs. Watne is now confined to a wheelchair, but she discovered her gift years previously. Now she thanks God that her present condition gives her more time to pray.[14] Spending that much time in prayer on a regular basis is beyond the possibilities of Christians who don't have the gift. If the truth were known I think we would all be surprised at the little amount of time American Christians spend in prayer. But for those who have the gift it's the most enjoyable thing in the world. "It's work," says Don Carlson, one of the Campus Crusade prayer staff. "Sit down sometime and pray for an hour. You'll find that it's mentally and physically demanding. But I love it!"

The life of Rees Howells, a Welsh coal miner who was

given the gift of intercession, is instructive reading for those who might want to learn more about intercession. It was written by Norman Grubb and titled, *Rees Howells: Intercessor*. In it Grubb points out that an intercessor is something more than an ordinary Christian who intensifies his or her prayer life. Intercession involves a combination of identification, agony and authority that those without the gift can seldom if ever experience or even identify with.[15]

Creative ways of harnessing the gift of intercession for church growth are yet to be discovered. Perhaps a start has been made, however, by Archie Parrish, director of Evangelism Explosion International. In Coral Ridge Presbyterian Church, Fort Lauderdale, Florida, a large and growing church, the Evangelism Explosion program has always been a potent force for outreach and growth. But in 1976 a further improvement was introduced that worked so well it is now being recommended to all churches which use Evangelism Explosion. Two church members who are not on the Evangelism Explosion team were asked to volunteer to pray for each Evangelism Explosion worker on a regular basis but especially on Tuesday night when the workers were out witnessing. The evangelist was responsible to get in touch with the two intercessors each week to report the results and give prayer requests. When this started the number of professions of faith immediately went up 100 percent!

There is a power in prayer for church growth. Thousands who have a special gift to do it need to discover, develop and use their gift. When they do, other gifted people will find themselves that much more effective, and the Body will grow.

Hyphenated Gifts

Some books on spiritual gifts make a strong point that

in Ephesians 4:11 the gifts most often listed as "pastor" and "teacher" should be written "pastor-teacher." William McRae, for example, says, "This gift is the only dual gift in the New Testament. There are not two gifts here. It is one gift which has two distinct dimensions."[16] This is probably correct, at least in the translation that best reflects the sense of the Greek text.

In an open-ended approach to spiritual gifts, however, it is best not to think that this is the only hyphenated gift at work in the Body of Christ. Because pastor-teacher is indeed a very common combination of gifts, it stands as our prototype. Most scholars would admit that teacher can stand alone as a gift because it does in some of the other lists. But this is the only list that mentions pastor and it is combined here with teacher. Furthermore, in a sense a pastor has to be "apt to teach" (1 Tim. 3:2). But whether all of this means that every pastor needs the gift of teaching to go along with his or her pastoral gift is questionable.

As we discuss the gifts in context, I will mention several other hyphenated gifts such as intercession-healing, tongues-interpretation, giving-voluntary poverty, scholar-teacher, and so forth. But at this point we simply needed to become familiar with the concept.

Variations and Degrees of Gifts

Within almost every one of the 27 spiritual gifts exists a wide range of variations and degrees. The cue for this might be seen in 1 Corinthians 12:4-6 when it speaks of gifts *(charismaton)*, ministries *(diakonion)*, and workings *(energematon)*. Ray Stedman defines ministry as "the sphere in which a gift is performed," and a working as "the degree of power by which a gift is manifested or ministered on a specific occasion."[17]

A person with the gift of evangelist, for example,

might be a personal evangelist or a public evangelist—different variations of the gift. One public evangelist might be an international celebrity who fills stadiums of 50,000 people and sees 3,000 conversions in a week. Another public evangelist, with a lesser degree of the gift, might minister mostly in churches that hold 500 and see 30 conversions in a week. In the final analysis, both may be found to be equally faithful in the exercise of their gift.

Variations and degrees, like the gifts themselves, are distributed at the discretion of God. Just as the master in the parable of the talents gave to one five talents, to another two and to yet another one, so God in His wisdom gives to each of us a "measure of faith" (Rom. 12:3). This is why, when gifts are properly in operation, there is no cause for jealousy or envy even among Christians who have different degrees of the same gift. My left hand is not envious of my right hand because it may not be able to develop skills equal to my right hand. Rather the two hands work together harmoniously for the benefit of the whole body. God has given me a gift for writing, for example, but I am also realistic enough to know that scores of others such as David Hubbard and Martin Marty and Betty Elliot and John Stott, to name a few, have such a high degree of the gift that I am not worthy to change their typewriter ribbons. I thank God for all of them and for the tremendous contribution they are making to the Body of Christ. And I try to add my small contribution as well.

Classifying the Gifts

There are many different ways of classifying the gifts. Some classical Pentecostals speak of *the* nine gifts of the Spirit and use the list in 1 Corinthians 12:8-10. Bill Gothard divides them into motivations, ministries, and manifestations. David Hocking uses speaking gifts, serving gifts, and supernatural gifts.[18] Some of the Reformed theologians of the past separated ordinary gifts from extraordinary gifts. Kenneth Kinghorn recognizes enabling gifts, servicing gifts, and tongues/ interpretation.[19] William Baird likes pedagogical gifts, supernatural gifts and gifts of special communication.[20] Jack MacGorman's choice is intelligible utterance, power, spiritual discernment, and ecstatic utterance.[21] Many others could be added.

Some of the people mentioned above have had excellent success in teaching Christians to discover, develop and use their spiritual gifts. I applaud whatever classification they use if it works. It is quite obvious that there is no divinely inspired biblical classification. So I say, if it works for you and your people, use it.

In my own teaching, as reflected in this book, I prefer the open-ended approach to classifying gifts. The reason I have chosen it is not because I think it is any more biblical than the others, but because I have found it to be the most helpful approach for my own particular teaching style. It works for me, and it may work for some others as well.

Churches Have "Gift-Mixes" Too

The philosophy of ministry of many local churches and that of certain whole denominations includes a particular position on spiritual gifts. One of the most frequent is the conviction that the "sign gifts" ceased with the age of the apostles. I have traced some of the history of this viewpoint in the introduction, but here I need to stress that it remains a delicate point of debate today. In fact probably no other aspect of the doctrine of spiritual gifts has caused as much dissension, church-splitting, and polemical exchanges as this issue.

I am impressed that there are such wonderful Christian leaders on both sides. Merrill Unger argues that the "sign gifts" of healing, working of miracles, tongues, interpretation, work of knowledge, prophecy, and apostle are no longer needed in our churches.[22] John Walvoord's list of gifts that have passed away includes apostleship, prophecy, miracles, healing, tongues, interpretation, and discerning spirits.[23] John Stott would exclude apostles and prophets and possibly workers of miracles.[24] John MacArthur feels that the temporary gifts are miracles, healing, tongues and interpretation.[25] David Hocking teaches that the gifts no longer functioning are prophecy, miracles, faith, healings, tongues, interpretation, word of knowledge, word of wisdom, and discerning of spirits.[26]

Leaders who take the contrary position, that the gifts mentioned above are in operation today, include as equally an impressive list of blue-chip evangelicals. Among them are Leslie Flynn, B.E. Underwood, Donald Gee, Rick Yohn, Kenneth Kinghorn, Charles Hummel, and others. Michael Griffiths argues the point strongly and hints that the dispensational position is uncomfortably close to being a form of liberalism.[27]

Some have been on both sides. Dr. Earl Radmacher, president of Western Conservative Baptist Seminary, was brought up in the Pentecostal tradition but has left it and now firmly opposes the use of tongues in the churches. Dr. Rodman Williams, a Presbyterian scholar who formerly took the Warfield view that miraculous gifts had ceased, is now president of Melodyland School of Theology. A convinced charismatic, Williams says, "Now we wonder how we could have misread the New Testament for so long!"[28]

Two of my favorite churches are located nearby in the San Fernando Valley. I attended one of them, Grace

Community Church of the Valley, on a Sunday morning when Pastor John MacArthur was preaching the first message in a series entitled, "What Is Wrong with the Charismatic Movement." On another Sunday I attended the Church on the Way and heard Pastor Jack Hayford give a message in tongues and interpret it right in the worship service. Both churches are growing at phenomenal rates. One has a Sunday attendance of 5,000; the other 3,000. Both have members who dearly love Jesus Christ, who want to serve Him, and who are growing in their faith. Both believe in and practice spiritual gifts. Yet they disagree as to which of the gifts ought to be in use in churches today.

My studies of the growing churches in America have not led me to believe that the question of which spiritual gifts are or are not now in effect is a primary growth factor. Much more important seems to be the recognition that the Holy Spirit is working through gifts and that Christians need to discover, develop and use them.

How is all this explained, then? My own conclusion is that just as God gives specific gift-mixes to different people, He also gives specific gift-mixes to different churches and denominations. The gift-mix a church or denomination has should be one of the determining factors of their philosophy of ministry. Churches with different philosophies of ministry are a part of the beautiful variety that God has built into the universal Body of Christ. Because people are so different, churches also need to be different if they are going to win unbelievers to Christ and fold them into responsible membership. In no way would I suggest that the philosophies of ministry of Grace Community or Church on the Way change. In my opinion, God loves them equally and His blessing on both is evident.

As far as church growth is concerned, establishing a

firm philosophy of ministry should be a very high priority. Each church needs to be able to articulate just what it stands for and what makes it different from other churches in the area. This is a sign of strength. The less frequently a philosophy of ministry is revised, the more potential for growth a church has.

What do I say, then, to a church that has a philosophy of ministry which excludes the sign gifts? Obviously, my own personal preference is broader than that, and therefore I belong to a church that has a broader philosophy of ministry. But for me, church growth principles are above personal preference, so I do not try to impose my views on others.

To illustrate, some months ago I was privileged to speak on spiritual gifts and church growth to virtually all the district superintendents of the Church of the Nazarene, as fine a roomful of Christian leaders that one could find. It so happens that the Church of the Nazarene is thoroughly convinced as a denomination that tongues is a gift which ought not be practiced in churches today. My advice to them was to interpret their position on spiritual gifts as from God and to stick to it.

Perhaps no two churches or denominations need the same gift-mix. God has given the Church of the Nazarene a gift-mix different from that of the Assemblies of God, and the Seventh-Day Adventists and the Christian and Missionary Alliance. If their mix has been determined by God, He can and will bless them, as long as they decide to discover, develop and use their gifts that they feel God has given them. Nothing else is necessary. They would be unwise to spend the time and energy required to battle through a change in their philosophy of ministry.

As to the individual church, I suggest that if, for reasons considered valid and biblical by the leadership of the church, tongues and/or other gifts are not considered legitimate, the church would do well to take a cue from a Conservative Baptist church in Arizona I heard about. The pastor of this church "stated, in a positive but firm way, that when people came into his church they noticed the name 'Baptist' over the front door. He further stated that Baptists do not believe in or practice speaking in tongues and that he did not want to argue the case with them. However, if this was their practice, he felt they would be happier in a church where this practice was acceptable, and he respectfully suggests they search for such a church."[29]

Let me add parenthetically that while this is the position of most *Conservative* Baptists, some other kinds of Baptists do have different gift-mixes and many are open to charismatic manifestations such as tongues.

But the principle remains. If it is God who distributes the gifts both to churches and to individuals, churches and denominations will do well to accept what God has given them without pride or envy or guilt or self-consciousness or a feeling of inferiority. Whatever the gift-mix God has chosen for you and your church, it is a mix adequate for growth if the dynamic is released by the power of the Holy Spirit and in obedience to the Lord of the harvest.

Notes

1. Lawrence J. Peter and Raymond Hull, *The Peter Principle* (New York: Bantam Books, 1969), p. 7.
2. Festo Kivengere, *I Love Idi Amin* (Old Tappan, NJ: Fleming H. Revell Co., 1977).
3. Jean Dye Johnson, *God Planted Five Seeds* (New York· Harper and Row, Publishers, Inc., 1966).
4. I told this story briefly in the preface to the first edition of *Defeat of the Bird God* (Grand Rapids: Zondervan Publishing House, 1967), but the preface was not reprinted when the William Carey Library edition was printed later.

5. Leslie B. Flynn, *Nineteen Gifts of the Spirit* (Wheaton: Victor Books, 1974), p. 10.
6. David Mains, *Full Circle* (Waco: Word Books, 1971).
7. Karen Mains, *Open Heart, Open Home* (Elgin: David C. Cook, Publishing Co., 1976).
8. Karen Mains, "Hospitality Means More Than a Party," *Moody Monthly* (December, 1976), p. 38. Another article on Karen Mains was written by Ron Wilson, "Open Hearted Living," *Christian Life* (July, 1976), pp. 26ff.
9. Edith Schaeffer, "Hospitality: Optional or Commanded?" *Christianity Today* (December 17, 1976), pp. 28,29.
10. A careful study of the use of hospitality by early Christians was done by Donald Wayne Riddle, "Early Christian Hospitality: A Factor in the Gospel Transmission," *Journal of Biblical Literature* (vol. 57, 1938). pp. 141-154.
11. "A Man with a Vision," *Christian Life* (March, 1978), p. 21.
12. Elizabeth O'Connor, *Eighth Day of Creation* (Waco, Word Books, 1971), p. 32.
13. Bryan Pollock, "Have You Ever Tried to Pray (For Eight Hours a Day)?" *Worldwide Challenge* (January, 1978), pp. 12-14.
14. Wanda Dugan, "She May Have Prayed for You," *Worldwide Challenge* (October, 1977), pp. 26-29.
15. Norman Grubb, *Rees Howells: Intercessor* (Fort Washington, PA: Christian Literature Crusade, 1973), p. 86.
16. William J. McRae, *The Dynamics of Spiritual Gifts* (Grand Rapids: Zondervan Publishing House, 1976), p. 59.
17. Ray C. Stedman, *Body Life* (Glendale: Regal Books, 1972), pp. 40,41.
18. David L. Hocking, *Spiritual Gifts: Their Necessity and Use in the Local Church* (Long Beach, CA: Sounds of Grace, n.d.), pp. 52,53.
19. Kenneth Cain Kinghorn, *Gifts of the Spirit* (Nashville: Abingdon Press, 1976), p. 41.
20. Jack W. MacGorman, *The Gifts of the Spirit* (Nashville: Broadman Press, 1974), pp. 34,35.
21. *Ibid*.
22. Merrill F. Unger, *The Baptism and Gifts of the Holy Spirit* (Chicago: Moody Press, 1974), p. 139.
23. John F. Walvoord, *The Holy Spirit* (Grand Rapids: Zondervan Publishing House, 1954), pp. 173-188.
24. John R.W. Stott, *One People* (Downers Grove: Inter-Varsity Press, 1968), p. 27. See also Stott's work, *Baptism and Fullness: The Work of the Holy Spirit Today* (Downers Grove: Inter-Varsity Press, 1976), pp. 94-102.
25. John MacArthur, Jr., *The Church—the Body of Christ* (Grand Rapids: Zondervan Publishing House, 1973), p. 150.
26. David Hocking, *Spiritual Gifts*, p. 51.
27. Michael Griffiths, *Cinderella's Bethrothal Gifts* (Robesonia, PA: OMF Books, 1978), p. 8.
28. J. Rodman Williams, *The Era of the Spirit* (Plainfield, NJ: Logos International, 1971), p. 28.
29. *Arizona Baptist*, "Charismatics in a Baptist Church," March, 1978, p. 4.

3.
Four Things That Gifts Are Not

As an important aspect of dispelling ignorance about spiritual gifts, we must be sure that no confusion exists in certain areas which have tended to throw some people off the track. In my experience I have come across four of these areas which need special attention. Spiritual gifts are often confused with natural talents, fruit of the Spirit, Christian roles and, to some extent, counterfeit gifts.

Let's look at these one at a time.

Don't Confuse Spiritual Gifts with Natural Talents

Every human being, by virtue of being made in the image of God, possesses certain natural talents. As with spiritual gifts, there are obviously different variations and degrees among the natural talents. Talents are one of the features that give every human being a unique personality. Part of our self-identity has to be the particular mix of talents that we have.

Where do these natural talents come from? Ultimately, they are given by God, and as such they should be recognized in a sense as gifts. That's why we often say of a person who sings well or has an extraordinary IQ or who can hit a golf ball into a hole from a long distance, "My, isn't that person gifted?"

Having natural talents has nothing directly to do with being a Christian or being a member of the Body of Christ. Many atheists, for example, have superb talent for one thing or another. They have natural talents but they do not have spiritual gifts.

Christians, like anyone else, also have natural talents. But they should not be confused with spiritual gifts. It is usually incorrect for a Christian to say that his or her gift is fixing automobiles, gourmet cooking, telling jokes, painting pictures, or playing basketball.

To make matters worse, the biblical word *charisma* has been secularized. I understand from Greek scholars that the word is almost exclusively used by the apostle Paul in Greek literature. The only other two appearances are in 1 Peter 4:10 and once in Philo's writings. But a century ago the famous German sociologist, Max Weber, began to use the word in terms of a certain kind of leader which he called a "charismatic leader." In that sense the word is now used of Anwar Sadat or Henry Kissinger or Fidel Castro, to name a few international figures who obviously are "charismatic" in the broad sense of the word. But none of the three, as far as I know, is a member of the Body of Christ, and thus none of them has been given a spiritual gift.

Spiritual gifts are reserved exclusively for Christians. No unbeliever has one, and every true believer in Jesus does. Spiritual gifts are not to be regarded as dedicated natural talents. There may be a discernible relationship between the two, however, because in some cases (not all, by any means) God takes a natural talent in an unbeliever and transforms it into a spiritual gift when that person enters the Body of Christ. But even in a case like this, the spiritual gift is more than just a souped-up natural talent. Because it is given by God, a spiritual gift can never be cloned.

One of the most vivid cases I know of involves my good friend and colleague, John Wimber, the founder of the Church Growth Department of Fuller Evangelistic Association. Before John became a Christian about 15 years ago, he had two outstanding natural talents. First, he was an accomplished musician. He played all instruments, wrote music, arranged music, directed groups, and studied music theory on a graduate level. Secondly, he was a good salesman. He was extremely successful in marketing music. He owned music stores, managed groups on tour, made records and had an income so high he might be embarrassed if I mentioned the amount in print.

When John Wimber became a Christian through a dramatic conversion experience that reminds one of the apostle Paul's, God did an interesting thing with the natural talents. John's musical talent apparently has never been transformed into a spiritual gift. The talent remained, and he dedicated it to God, and composed some hymns and sang occasionally to the glory of God. But not much more. God had something else in mind for him.

When John Wimber became a member of the Body of Christ, God took his natural talent as a salesman and transformed that into the gift of evangelist. As a result, over 2,000 people who are now living in Orange County,

California will tell you that John Wimber is their spiritual father. Not only did God give him the gift of evangelist, but he gave it in a high degree. Through his gift, John gets an intuitive feeling that tells him when an unbeliever is ready to be born again. He says that he feels like a spiritual midwife. He knows when the time has come and he knows how to make the delivery. When John Wimber doesn't lead several people to Christ in a week, he gets restless and feels like there's something wrong.

Don't Confuse Spiritual Gifts with the Fruit of the Spirit

The fruit of the Spirit is described in Galatians 5:22, 23. Love, joy, peace, longsuffering, gentleness, goodness, faith, meekness, and self-control (temperance) are listed there. Some Bible expositors point out the fact that "fruit" is in the singular, and that the original Greek construction would permit a colon after love. So, while all these other things are part of the fruit, love is probably the primary one.

It is improper to speak of the "gift of love," if by gift you mean that love should become spiritual gift number 28 on our list. In the broad sense, of course, love is a gift from God and should be so regarded. "We love [God] because he first loved us" (1 John 4:19). But love is not a *charisma* in the sense that God gives it to some members of the Body, but not to others.

The fruit of the Spirit is the normal, expected outcome of Christian growth, maturity, Christlikeness, and fullness of the Holy Spirit. Since all Christians have the responsibility of growing in their faith, all have the responsibility of developing the fruit of the Spirit. Fruit is not discovered like the gifts, it is developed through the believer's walk with God and through yieldedness to the Holy Spirit. While spiritual gifts help define what a Christian *does*, the fruit of the Spirit helps define what a Christian *is*.

The fruit of the Spirit is a prerequisite for the effective exercise of spiritual gifts. Gifts without fruit are worthless. The Corinthian believers found this out the hard way. They had an ideal gift-mix, according to 1 Corinthians 1:7. They were busy discovering, developing and using their spiritual gifts. They were as charismatic as a church can get. Yet they were a spiritual disaster area, one of the most messed up churches you can read about in the New Testament.

Their basic problem was not gifts, it was fruit. That is why Paul wrote 1 Corinthians 13 to them. In it, he waxed eloquently about love, the fruit of the Spirit. He told them that they could have the gift of tongues, the gift of prophecy, the gift of knowledge, the gift of faith, the gift of voluntary poverty, the gift of martyrdom and any other gift, but without love they amounted to absolutely nothing (see 1 Cor. 13:1-3). Gifts without fruit are like an automobile tire without air—the ingredients are all there, but they are worthless.

Also, gifts are temporal but fruit is eternal. In the same chapter we are told that gifts such as prophecy and tongues and knowledge shall vanish away. But faith, hope and love will abide. Whereas gifts are task-oriented, fruit is God-oriented.

It is worth noting that a passage on fruit accompanies every one of the primary passages on gifts. First Corinthians 13 is the most explicit and most widely recognized. But also, the list of gifts ending in Romans 12:8 is immediately followed by "let love be without hypocrisy" and "be kindly affectioned one to another with brotherly love" (Rom. 12:9,10). The passage continues for another 11 verses. Then in Ephesians 4, the gift passage ends with verse 16 and the fruit passage picks up in the next verse and carries through the next chapter. Among other things it says, "Walk in love, as Christ also hath loved us" (Eph. 5:2). The passage on spiritual gifts beginning with 1 Peter 4:9 is immediately preceded with "above all things have fervent [love] among yourselves: for [love] shall cover the multitude of sins" (1 Pet. 4:8).

Don't Confuse Spiritual Gifts with Christian Roles

When you look over the list of 27 spiritual gifts, it becomes obvious that many of them describe activities that are expected of every Christian. At this point it is very helpful to distinguish between spiritual gifts and Christian roles. Roles are slightly different from the fruit of the Spirit in that they involve more doing than being. But they are similar to the fruit in that they are expected of every Christian.

Perhaps the most obvious spiritual gift that is also a Christian role is faith. Just becoming a Christian and first entering into the Body of Christ requires faith. And this faith, according to the Bible, is a gift of God (see Eph. 2:8,9). Then we are told that faith is a part of the fruit of the Spirit (see Gal. 5:22), and that "without faith it is impossible to please [God]" (Heb. 11:6). In other words, the life-style of every Christian without exception is to be characterized by day in and day out faith. Over and above this, however, is the special gift of faith that is given by God to only a few members of the Body. This will be described in some detail later on. But the gift of faith is much more than the fruit of faith and role of faith which we see in an ordinary Christian.

While discussing the gift of hospitality in the last chapter, I mentioned that neither Doris nor I has the gift. However, we do have a role of entertaining guests, and we do it with some regularity. Having people over for dinner, occasionally putting a person up for the night, taking a visitor out, hosting church parties, loaning our car, making sure that new people are oriented to the community are all included in our Christian role. None of these things comes easily and we never feel that we do as much of it or do it as well as we should. But we do make an effort.

Prayer is both a privilege and a responsibility of every Christian. It is another example of a Christian role. One does not need the gift of intercession to talk to God. Likewise, some have the gift of ministry or serving, but all Christians should serve one another (see Gal. 5:13). Some have the gift of exhortation, but all have a general role of exhorting one another (see Heb. 10:25). A few have the gift of evangelist, but all Christians are expected to exercise their role of witness (see Acts 1:8).

The role of celibacy is an important one to stress in our contemporary permissive society when some people are trying to establish a "new morality." In the discussion of the gift of celibacy, I indicated that I did not have the gift and have worked this out by being married. But I do have a role of celibacy that I particularly need to exercise when I am traveling away from home. Opportunities for unfaithfulness are usually not lacking if one is looking for them. I recall one unusual occasion in a rural hotel in Taiwan where, without my knowledge, the hotel manager had already assigned a sleeping partner to my room. I must admit that when I took a look at her there was no real temptation involved, but there could have been. And in any case I was responsible to God to exercise my role of celibacy, which I did.

By the same token, the role of celibacy is very apropos to Christians who have not yet married and to men and women who have lost a spouse through death or divorce. Most of the latter have already discovered that they do not have the gift of celibacy, and yet there is a way to be a Christian widow or divorcee and maintain continence until God provides another partner. Not having the gift is no excuse to sin.

Christians need to be ready to exercise any role in case of emergency or need. When an accident occurs you help the victim as much as you can until the doctor arrives. When a fire starts you put as much of it out as you can until the fire department arrives. Many Christians are spared frequent situations such as these in their spiritual lives, but some, pastors of churches for example, find themselves having to use roles all the time simply because the need is there and someone has to fill it whether they have special gifts or not.

I once spoke about spiritual gifts at a church and in my presentation mentioned that gifts are distributed in the Body of Christ much like assignments are distributed on a football team. I mentioned that offensive tackles don't make touchdowns and get their names in the headlines, but without them the team would lose because the running backs couldn't make touchdowns either. After the meeting a big man came up to me and told me he had played offensive tackle in college. I asked him if he ever made a touchdown. He smiled a broad smile and said that he had made one once. It was a freak play and he was one of the very few tackles in the NCAA ever to make a touchdown. But when the ball popped loose he stopped blocking, grabbed it and started running. His "gift," in this analogy, was blocking but in running he was exercising a role, just as Christians must when such an opportunity arises.

Gift 5: The Gift of Giving

The way Christian roles operate alongside spiritual

gifts is vividly illustrated by the gift of giving.

There is no question that every Christian is to give part of his or her income to the Lord. According to the Bible, every person should set definite giving goals and give with cheerfulness (see 2 Cor. 9:7). This is a Christian role, and there are no exceptions. Rich Christians should give and poor Christians should give. Young marrieds who have low incomes and high expenses should give alongside more mature people who are financially secure. New Christians should be taught to give as soon as they begin growing in their faith.

How much should Christians give?

As I read the Scriptures, I have to conclude that a tithe, meaning 10 percent of one's income off the top, is the bare minimum for exercising the role of giving. I am not ordinarily legalistic in my views of Christian behavior, but I have to say that I believe that anyone who is under the 10 percent figure is engaging in a form of spiritual cheating. Some cheat the I.R.S. regularly and get away with it. No one cheats God and gets away with it. "Be not deceived; God is not mocked; for whatsoever a man soweth, that shall he also reap" (Gal. 6:7).

It is a well-known fact that a large number of Christians are not exercising their role of giving. The average giving for Christians in America is something around $145 per year. The average salary is considerably more than $1,450. My church, Lake Avenue Congregational Church, is a fairly affluent church, basically upper-middle class. However I once figured that if all our members received California welfare payments and tithed, our income would go up by 40 percent! I was disappointed to see in the paper that the person considered to be America's No. 1 evangelical Christian, President Jimmy Carter, apparently does not tithe. His taxable income in 1975, was $122,189, and his church giving was only

$6,000 or 4.9 percent. In any case it was considerably better than President Nixon who, in 1969, gave $250 to his church which figures to less than $5.00 per week.

I began taking the role of giving seriously when, three years ago, our pastor, Raymond Ortlund, preached an exceptionally good stewardship sermon during our November fund-raising drive. Among other things, he told us that he and his wife gave 25 percent off the top. My wife and I did some calculating and found that we were barely scraping the 10 percent. So we prayed and decided to try to raise our giving by a couple of percentage points a year until we got to 15 percent. Then we would pray again. During the process we discovered that the Scripture, "Give, and it shall be given unto you; good measure, pressed down, and shaken together, and running over" (Luke 6:38) is literally true. We have passed the 15 percent and now feel that financially we couldn't afford to drop back to where we were before. It works so well that I have yet to meet a Christian who started to tithe and then went back to not tithing. Apart from faithfulness to God, it is simply not good business sense.

I have said all this to say that my wife and I do not have the gift of giving. I believe I am not falling into the trap of gift projection by saying that, but simply describing a Christian role. In fact, I am becoming more convinced that the only route to go in an affluent society such as we have here in America is to agree as Christians on a graduated tithe—the more you make the more percentage you give. Ronald Sider advocates this in a recent book and I certainly agree with him.[1]

The reason I am convinced that my wife and I do not have the gift of giving is because we keep asking ourselves the question: how much can we give to the Lord? Christians who have the gift of giving do not ask this.

They use another, quite different basic question. I learned that question from the late R.G. LeTourneau.

R.G. LeTourneau, the great Texas industrialist, had the gift of giving. The key question is described in his autobiography. In it he said, "The question is not how much of my money I give to God, but rather how much of God's money I keep."[2] He answered it in his life by turning 90 percent of the assets of the company over to his Christian foundation, and then he and his wife gave in cash 90 percent of the income that was realized from the share of the business that he kept. He and his wife never lacked.

A more contemporary Christian brother with the gift of giving is Stanley Tam who is in the silver business in Lima, Ohio. He made God the senior partner of his business by legally turning 51 percent over to his Christian foundation, then raising it over a period of time to 100 percent. The foundation receives the profits from the business. It almost goes without saying that he and his wife tithe their own family income as well. Without using the exact words, Stanley Tam recognizes his unusual ability to give to the Lord as a spiritual gift. He makes a point of avoiding the temptation of gift projection. He says in his autobiography, "I frankly don't believe I'm as good a businessman as our financial statements indicate. I believe I operate far above my natural capacity."[3] In another place he is careful to say, "Let me urge you not to use me as an example . . . God has made what might be called singular demands on my life. He may do the same to you or choose to orient and motivate you in completely different ways."[4]

Although such highly successful people as LeTourneau and Tam are usually the ones recognized and given as examples in books like this, the gift of giving is given to lower income people as well. The apostle Paul mentions the Christians in Macedonia who gave out of their poverty (see 2 Cor. 8:1,2). Jesus' comment that the widow's mite was more than the rich people gave is well-known (see Mark 12:41-44). James McCormick, who has a construction business in Birmingham, Alabama, is now a millionaire. But he discovered his gift of giving while he was working in a clothing store and making $35 a week. At that time he made a promise to give 50 percent of his income to the Lord and has been doing so ever since. There is no question that the $17.50 per week he gave then was worth just as much to God as the very sizable amounts that James McCormick gives now.[5]

The gift of giving is the special ability God gives to certain members of the Body of Christ to contribute their material resources to the work of the Lord with liberality and cheerfulness.

Gift 22: The Gift of Voluntary Poverty

I am indebted to Donald Bridge and David Phypers for bringing the gift of voluntary poverty to my attention.[6] Its biblical reference is in 1 Corinthians 13:3, "Though I bestow all my goods to feed the poor . . . ." For years I simply assumed that this was another way of describing the gift of giving, but now I understand that it is different although often related. Probably everyone who has the gift of voluntary poverty also has the gift of giving. However, not all who have the gift of giving have the corresponding gift of voluntary poverty.

The gift of voluntary poverty is the special ability that God gives to certain members of the Body of Christ to renounce material comfort and luxury and adopt a personal life-style equivalent to those living at the poverty level in a given society in order to serve God more effectively.

The use of the adjective "voluntary" is important here to separate those with the gift from those who find themselves poverty-stricken because of uncontrollable social circumstances. Furthermore, it must be recognized that wealth and poverty are only relative terms. Poor, yes, but compared to what? When we first began to think through the implications of this gift, Doris and I wondered if we might have had the gift when we were missionaries. After all, in 1971, the last year we were on the field, the total income for our family of five was $3,900. If we made this here in America's economy we certainly would consider ourselves poor. But while in Bolivia we were able to live considerably above the poverty level on that kind of budget. We had to admit that we did not have the gift.

John Wesley, however, did have the hyphenated gift of giving-voluntary poverty. When he died he left a well-worn frock coat and two silver teaspoons in his estate. But during his lifetime he had given $150,000 to the Lord.[7]

George Muller of Bristol was another. He died with a total personal estate of $850. He was a poor man all his life. Yet, when his books were audited after his death it was discovered much to everyone's surprise that through the years a total of $180,000 had been given by a donor identified only as "a servant of the Lord Jesus, who, constrained by the love of Christ, seeks to lay up treasure in heaven." The donor of course was Mr. Muller himself.[8]

John Wesley and George Muller stand in contrast to R.G. LeTourneau and Stanley Tam, who exercise the gift of giving without that of voluntary poverty. I appreciate Stanley Tam's open statement that "I like good food, a comfortable house, decent clothes, a good car."[9] In fact it is likely that God has called Tam to be rich instead of poor so he can better exercise the gift of giving. Tam frankly says, "I have an insatiable thirst to make money. I love it. I like to promote, to see the company grow. I study our yearly and interim reports like a hungry hawk, evaluating, discovering, making checks and counterchecks."[10]

Such an attitude is quite out of keeping with the kind of thing that another group of American Christians who call themselves the People's Christian Coalition are doing. They exercise their gift of voluntary poverty by choosing to live a simple life-style in a commune in the poor section of Washington D.C. They are doing a wonderful thing in using their gifts to contribute to the well-being of the poor and oppressed in Washington's ghetto. The public statements published in their magazine, *Sojourners*, however, come close to the syndrome of gift projection. They spend a good deal of time attempting to produce biblical reasons why the kind of radical life-style they have developed might be more pleasing to God than the life-style of other Christians in our society who have and are exercising other spiritual gifts, but who are living at a more comfortable economic level. They associate such people with the "establishment" which is blamed for a variety of social and economic evils.

Perhaps this harshly critical attitude is due to the presence of another gift, that of prophecy. Writings in *Sojourners* have a ring of pessimism to them reminiscent of Jeremiah or others of the Old Testament prophets. Because of their gift-mix these radical evangelicals would probably feel as uncomfortable living in Billy Graham's secluded estate on Black Mountain in North Carolina or in Robert Schuller's commodious home in Orange, California, as Billy Graham or Robert Schuller would feel living in a commune in Washington's ghetto.

But "the eye cannot say unto the hand, I have no need of thee" (1 Cor. 12:21). Neither can or should any members of the Body with one gift-mix stand in harsh judgment of other members of the Body with another gift-mix. Perhaps, however, those with a certain variety of the gift of prophecy can't help it and need to be understood in that light by those of the so-called "establishment."

Well-spent money can be a tremendous stimulus to church growth. Much growth both here in America and among the unreached peoples of the world is now retarded because of lack of funds. It is estimated that there are 40 million evangelicals in America. Presumably evangelicals are concerned with spreading the faith around the world. But the national giving to missions totals about $750 million or an average of 36 cents per week per evangelical.

I would hope that, with all the current interest in spiritual gifts, thousands of believers will discover that God has given them the gift of giving and millions who are not now exercising their Christian role of giving will start doing so responsibly. The resources thus released for the spread of the gospel and the care of the suffering and oppressed would be incredible. God, I believe, would be highly pleased.

Don't Confuse Spiritual Gifts with Counterfeit Gifts

I wish I didn't have to write this section on counterfeit gifts. I wish it weren't true that Satan and his demons and evil spirits are real and actively opposing the work of the Lord. Jesus Himself said, "For there shall arise false Christs, and false prophets, and shall show great signs and wonders; insomuch that, if it were possible, they shall deceive the very elect" (Matt. 24:24). Jesus also speaks about those who prophesy and cast out demons in His name, but who, in reality, are workers of iniquity (see Matt. 7:22,23).

My wife and I consider ourselves fortunate that in 22 years of full-time Christian service, 16 of which were spent on the mission field, the Lord has never allowed us to come into firsthand contact with demons or spiritists or witchcraft or the occult. But we have many friends who have and who know what it is to be on the front lines in the battle against principalities and powers.

I do not doubt that Satan can counterfeit every gift on the list. He is a supernatural being and he has supernatural powers. His power was shown in a spectacular way in Egypt when Pharaoh's magicians could match practically all the works that God did through Moses (see Exod. 7—8). Of course, Satan's power is limited and controlled. I like the way Robert Tuttle puts it: "Satan is on a tether. If, however, we slip within reach or range of his tether, yielding to some particular temptation, he'll have us for breakfast."[11]

A rather chilling book on this subject called *The Challenging Counterfeit* was recently written by Raphael Gasson, now a Christian but formerly a spiritualist medium. He tells it like it is. I made the mistake of bringing it up at the supper table one night and ruined my daughter Becky's appetite. His experience has shown him that "It is very obvious that Satan is using an extremely subtle counterfeit to the precious gifts of the Spirit."[12] In his book he describes several of these counterfeits.

He specifically shows, for example, how the gifts of faith and miracles and healing and tongues and interpretation are produced by Satan. The counterfeit of the gift of discerning spirits he feels is clairvoyance and clairaudience. Even the gift of exorcism is cleverly reproduced by the devil.

Gasson recalls how Satan gave him the ability to prophesy, and points out that most of these counterfeit prophecies come true. That's one way that the devil makes his appeals more attractive. On one occasion during the war years, for example, a man brought Gasson an article belonging to his son who was in the service in order to find out where his son was. Through his spirit "guide" (who happened to be the spirit of an African witch doctor) Gasson found out that the owner of the article was well and a prisoner of war. The father then proceeded to show Gasson a telegram from the War Department stating that his son had been killed in action over two weeks previously. Gasson went back to his guide and verified that the soldier really was not dead and that the father would have this confirmed in three days. Sure enough, three days later the father got a telegram from the War Department apologizing for the mistake and saying that the boy was well and a prisoner of war.[13]

Some mistakenly interpret this kind of thing as a work of God. It is in reality the work of the devil. But it is no less real.

We immediately need to remind ourselves that God knows all about this and gives adequate power to His children to prevent it. Another of my colleagues on the Lausanne Committee for World Evangelization is Petrus Octavianus of Indonesia. On one occasion he was speaking to a huge audience of 3,000 people in Stuttgart, Germany. At the end of his presentation he asked for a time of silent prayer. When all was quiet, one man on the platform got up and began praying in tongues. Petrus Octavianus turned to him and in the name of Jesus commanded him to be silent. Octavianus later explained, "After I had prayed for clarity, it became clear to me that this speaking in tongues was not brought about by the Holy Spirit but by the enemy."[14]

I do not know if God has given Petrus Octavianus the gift of discerning of spirits but, if he does not have it, at that moment he was exercising one of those emergency Christian roles. It would be well at this point to take a brief look at the two spiritual gifts that most relate to this world of evil: discerning of spirits and exorcism.

Gift 13: The Gift of Discerning of Spirits

The New Testament clearly teaches that every Christian needs to be able to tell good from evil, right from wrong. Hebrews 5:14 says that mature Christians "have their senses exercised to discern both good and evil." The Berean Christians were commended for not being naive. They tested the preaching of the apostles against Scripture as we all must (see Acts 17:11). First John 4:1 is explicit in telling us to "believe not every spirit, but [test] the spirits whether they are of God."

These passages describe the Christian role of discernment. However, over and above what is expected of all Christians is a gift of discerning of spirits given to only a few. It is a gift that may not be exercised frequently. Those who have it may even be reluctant about using it because it requires a good deal of courage. But it is comforting for the whole Body to know that God has not left Christians defenseless against the tactics of Satan and his forces of evil.

The gift of discerning of spirits is the special ability God gives to some members of the Body of Christ which enables them to know with assurance whether certain behavior purported to be of God is in reality divine, human or satanic.

The apostle Peter apparently had this gift. He used it dramatically when he discerned that Satan had inspired Ananias to lie about his real estate deal, and Ananias was struck dead on the spot. He repeated it with Ananias' wife, Sapphira, who also died (see Acts 5:1-10). Later on in Samaria, Peter used the gift to see through to the heart motives of Simon the sorcerer. He had all the assurance from God he needed to tell Simon that he was "in the gall of bitterness, and in the bond of iniquity" (Acts 8:23).

The gift of discernment can operate on various levels. The most obvious is the ability to know that apparently good behavior is in reality the work of Satan. This is the level on which Petrus Octavianus was ministering in Stuttgart. Another level is that of discerning whether something a Christian brother or sister does emerges from godly motives or carnal motives. A third level involves the supernatural ability to distinguish truth from error, even when motives are proper. It goes without saying that the latter two involve very sensitive kinds of judgment and must be accompanied with an extra measure of the fruit of the Spirit if they are going to be helpful to the Body. Members of the Body with the gift of discernment are one thing. Self-styled heresy hunters are something else, and at times I think the American church is already overpopulated with them.

Gift 27: The Gift of Exorcism

While the gift of exorcism[15] is one of the gifts that is not mentioned in the Bible specifically as a *charisma*, there are abundant evidences that it was at work in the New Testament and that it is at work in our contemporary world.

The gift of exorcism is the special ability that God has given to certain members of the Body of Christ to cast out demons and evil spirits.

It is reasonable to believe that discernment-exorcism is another one of the hyphenated gifts such as pastor-teacher. They seemed to be operating together when the apostle Paul, for example, became annoyed with the young girl in Philippi who kept saying, "These men are servants of the most high God, which show unto us the way of salvation." These words don't sound like there is anything wrong with them. But Paul was able to discern that it was an evil spirit speaking through her, and he exorcised the spirit (see Acts 16:16-18).

Exorcism should not be practiced without the gift of discernment. Unfortunately there is in some circles today an excessive preoccupation with demons and evil spirits. Ralph Neighbour tells of one dear saint who was in a hotel hallway praying demons out of her doorknob because it was sticking.[16] We do not need large numbers of pop exorcists who do their thing with no reference to properly discerning the spirits. As Robert Tuttle says, "Those who would cast demons out of everything that wiggles could well endanger the weaker parts of the body of Christ. Those who are able to cast out evil spirits must not only approach such a ministry with extreme caution but only after much prayer and fasting and by the power of the Holy Spirit."[17]

One of the most dramatic cause-and-effect relationships between exorcism and church growth that I am aware of began right here in Pasadena. A young man from Bolivia, Julio Cesar Ruibal, was studying pre-med in Pasadena City College. On the side he happened to be the youngest and one of the two most powerful gurus of the occult in the western hemisphere. But God had His hand on him. He first heard the gospel in a Kathryn Kuhlman meeting and found himself very confused. The next day he attended a prayer meeting at the home of a charismatic couple from my church, Lake Avenue Congregational Church. Two ladies were there who had the gift of exorcism. In a spine-tingling testimony, Ruibal tells how he was delivered from the demons of yoga, clairvoyance, astrology, voodoo, reincarnation, the kabbala, levitation, metaphysical healing, automatic writing, use of the pendulum, extrasensory perception, and others. When the demons left they cast him on the floor and he says it felt like an electric current going out of his body.[18]

As Julio Cesar Ruibal grew in the Lord, he felt called to return to Bolivia to preach the gospel. By then he had discovered that he had the gift of healing. The meetings he held in Bolivia in 1973 turned out to be the most spectacular evangelistic meetings in that country before or since.[19] Thousands of people who found the Lord through his ministry in Bolivia (including President Banzer's wife) can thank the Lord also for the two ladies in Pasadena who had the gift of exorcism and who knew how to use it.

How Long Do You Keep Your Gift?

There is a common theory, prevalent in some circles, that every believer is eligible to use any gift at any time it is necessary. This idea, which might be called the "channel theory," suggests that gifts may be only temporary possessions which the Lord gives for a time and then drops.

There is a certain sense of validity to the channel theory that must be acknowledged. It is true that every Christian must be prepared at any time to be a channel for whatever God might want to do through him or her. I do not have the gift of healing, for example, but God sometime may choose to have me lay hands on a sick person and heal him miraculously. I would love to do it. I have prayed for many sick people and to date have seen no miracles. Part of my Christian role is to keep open to this spontaneous and unpredictable working of the Holy Spirit. But what the Spirit does in occasions like that must not be confused with spiritual gifts.

I firmly believe that once a person is given a proper spiritual gift, it is a lifetime possession. This rather dogmatic opinion is derived from Romans 12:4, where Paul establishes the analogy of the physical body as the hermeneutical key for understanding spiritual gifts. If spiritual gifts are to the Body of Christ as hands, tongues and other members are to the physical body, there is no question in my mind that once we know what our gift is, we can depend on keeping it. No way do I go to bed at night with any idea whatsoever that tomorrow my foot might wake up a kidney. Both the development of the spiritual gifts in the life of an individual Christian and the smooth operation of the Body of Christ as a whole depends on the same kind of confidence.

Knowing that we will keep our gift and be accountable for what we do with it at the judgment helps us to plan our lives. For one thing, it can keep us from expending too much energy in using interesting Christian roles at the expense of energy which could be used for the exercise of spiritual gifts. Church growth depends on an effective mobilization of all the members of a congregation for the work of the Lord. Research shows that the average active Christian layperson will give something between three and ten hours a week to the church and Christian work. A ten-hour-a-week church member is a gem—most are much lower than that, and it is unrealistic to plan for anything different.

In many churches, most of the hours available are taken up with morning and evening worship services, Sunday School, prayer meetings and small group meetings. For the majority of people, this is time for personal spiritual improvement, not for the exercise of spiritual gifts. The little time left over for using spiritual gifts should be carefully planned and structured. Activities that would divert energy from them should be kept to a minimum.

My rule of thumb is: spiritual gifts should be used in structured time, while Christian roles should be exercised casually. For example, I think that Stanley Tam, who has the gift of giving, should spend a good amount of his time on financial affairs, figuring out how he can make more money for the Lord. I myself, with only my role of giving at stake, should sort of let financial things take their own course and spend my time on exercising the gifts I do have. If I spent as much energy worrying about cash flow, investments, and business trends as Stanley Tam, it would be a sin.

Multi-gifted people may find that at certain periods of their ministry some of their gifts will be dominant and others subordinate. Their ranking order might vary as circumstances change. This does not mean that they lost a gift along the way.

At the same time, some gifts may become dormant against God's will. You may have a gift that you are supposed to be using but aren't. This seemed to be what Paul had in mind when he had to keep exhorting Timothy to "neglect not the gift" (1 Tim. 4:14) and "stir up the gift" (2 Tim. 1:6) and "do the work of an evangelist" (2 Tim. 4:5), assuming that evangelist was one of Timothy's spiritual gifts. Allowing gifts to become dormant that should be active is one of the ways we can "quench the Spirit," and that ought to be avoided at all costs.

To illustrate, I want to use a fable attributed to Pastor Charles Swindoll of the dynamic Evangelical Free Church of Fullerton, California:

A group of animals decided to improve their general welfare by starting a school. The curriculum included swimming, running, climbing and flying. The duck, an excellent swimmer, was deficient in other areas, so he majored in climbing, running and flying, much to the detriment of his swimming. The rabbit, a superior runner, was forced to spend so much of his time in other classes that he soon lost much of his famed speed. The squirrel, who had been rated "A" as a climber dropped to a "C" because his instructors spent hours trying to teach him to swim and fly. And the eagle was disciplined for soaring to the treetop when he had been told to learn how to climb, even though flying was most natural for him.[20]

What more needs to be said? Growing churches such as Evangelical Free, Fullerton understand the dynamic of spiritual gifts and plan their church programs to maximize their effectiveness. They have learned that it is counterproductive to chain people's energies in activities they are not gifted for. They concentrate on their strengths in order to give the Holy Spirit free rein. They know how to set priorities. And the church grows.

Notes

1. Ronald J. Sider, *Rich Christians in an Age of Hunger* (Downers Grove: Inter-Varsity Press, 1977), pp. 175-178.
2. R.G. LeTourneau, *Mover of Men and Mountains* (Chicago: Moody Press, 1972), p. 280.
3. Stanley Tam, *God Owns My Business* (Waco: Word Books, 1969), p. 62.
4. *Ibid.*, p. 3.
5. Reported in *Straight from the Shoulder*, News Bulletin of Haggai Institute (April-May, 1976), p. 4.
6. Donald Bridge and David Phypers, *Spiritual Gifts and the Church* (Downers Grove: Inter-Varsity Press, 1973), pp. 78-81.
7. Basil Miller, *George Muller: The Man of Faith* (Grand Rapids: Zondervan Publishing House, 1941), pp. 126,127.
8. *Ibid.*
9. Tam, *God Owns My Business*, p. 50.
10. *Ibid.*, p. 47.
11. Robert G. Tuttle, *The Partakers: Holy Spirit Power for Persevering Christians* (Nashville: Abingdon Press, 1974), p. 61.
12. Raphael Gasson, *The Challenging Counterfeit* (Plainfield, NJ: Logos Books, 1966), p. 90.

13. *Ibid.*, pp. 105,106.
14. Kurt E. Koch, *Charismatic Gifts* (Quebec: Association for Christian Evangelism, 1975), pp. 42,43.
15. I am using the word "exorcism" in a nontechnical sense. Some whose ministry has involved this gift like to point out a technical distinction between the Greek words *exorkizo*, to exorcise and *ekballo*, to cast out. See, for example, Kent Philpott and R.L. Hymers, *The Deliverance Book* (Van Nuys, CA: Bible Voice, Inc.,) pp. 19,20.
16. Ralph W. Neighbour, Jr., *This Gift Is Mine* (Nashville: Broadman Press, 1974), p. 55.
17. Tuttle, *The Partakers*, p. 61.
18. Ruibal's detailed testimony can be found in Nicky Cruz, *Satan on the Loose* (Old Tappan: Fleming H. Revell Co., 1973), pp. 134-143.
19. The Bolivia ministry of Ruibal was reported in *Christianity Today* (March 16,1973), p. 40.
20. *Daily Bread* (September 1, 1976).

4.
How I Found My Gifts and How You Can Find Yours

There is no chapter in the Bible that deals with finding gifts. Nowhere does Peter or Paul or James say, "And now, brethren, I would have you follow these steps to discover your spiritual gifts." The lack of such a passage has convinced some that discovering gifts is an improper pursuit for Christians. The arguments pro and con were discussed in chapter 1.

In my opinion the lack of such specific instructions in the Bible should not be a deterrent to setting forth practical, twentieth-century procedures for knowing and doing God's will. There is no chapter in the Bible that tells us how to draw up the constitution and bylaws for a local church or even what membership requirements for a local church should be. Nothing there tells us how to organize a missionary society or how to support missionaries. For centuries theologians and Bible students have been trying to figure out when and how Christians should be baptized. Most Christians don't find this new or unusual.

I am not intimidated. Neither are the authors of other current books on spiritual gifts. Many of the books mentioned in the introduction include chapters like this one on how to discover your gift.

As I read through these chapters recently, I found what might have been predicted: they are all different, but they are also largely the same. No author likes to lift someone else's outline and use it, so each one thinks up his own. But the procedure for finding gifts is surprisingly similar from author to author. This is comforting, because it does seem that a consensus has been emerging which will eventually tend to reduce confusion and increase effectiveness. In any case, we who are in the field of teaching spiritual gifts are much closer to agreement with each other on how to do it than those, for example, in the field of baptism.

I have been using the five steps, which I will describe here, for so many years that I don't know where they came from. I would like to think that they are original, but I am old enough now to understand what Solomon meant when he said, "There is no new thing under the sun" (Eccl. 1:9). I have been using these five steps in seminars for 10 or 15 years, and they do work. It has been gratifying to see them emerging in several other books, confirming to me that they have proved useful at least to some.

These steps will work only in certain cases. Perhaps yours is one of them. But perhaps someone else's suggestions may better fit your own situation. Sometimes just one sentence or one phrase that no one else has said quite that way will turn the trick. Consider what

I say here. If my suggestions don't make sense to you, though, don't give up. Leslie Flynn's chapter 21 is "How to Discover Your Gift"; Kenneth Kinghorn's chapter 7 is "Discovering Your Gifts"; William McRae's chapter 5 is "The Discovery of Your Gift"; and Rick Yohn's chapter 11 is "What Are Your Gifts?" Any one of these may say it better for you than I do.

The deep desire of all those who are teaching spiritual gifts is not that their method or any other specific method be followed. Their desire is to see the Body of Christ come alive with a new dynamic, a new freedom, a new power. When this happens, all of a sudden the church gains a new relevance to the community as a whole, and new people start finding Jesus Christ. All this ultimately results in church growth.

Four Fundamental Prerequisites

Before beginning to take the actual steps toward finding your gift, there are four fundamental prerequisites that need to characterize your life. Leave out any one of them, and you will have a very difficult, if not impossible, time discovering your gift.

First, you have to be a Christian. Spiritual gifts are given only to members of the Body of Christ. Unfortunately not all members of churches in America are truly members of the Body of Christ. Almost all churches, some more than others, have members who are not committed to Jesus Christ. They may attend with some regularity, put money in the offering, even belong to some boards or committees and teach Sunday School. But they have never come into that personal relationship with the Saviour that some call being born again or some call commitment to Christ or some call saved or some call converted. The name is much less important than the relationship with Jesus Christ.

When I go into a church, I cannot just assume that everyone there is ready for teaching on spiritual gifts. Some may need teaching on salvation first. If you have a question in your mind, ask yourself honestly whether you can say that you have become a new creature in Christ; that old things are passed away and that everything is become new, to paraphrase the words of 2 Corinthians 5:17. If the answer is no, postpone trying to discover your spiritual gift. Seek help on finding Christ as your personal Saviour and Lord. Pray sincerely to God and expect the Scripture to be fulfilled that says, "Seek, and ye shall find" (Matt. 7:7). Find a person who is a born-again Christian and ask for advice. The Bible says, "If thou shalt confess with thy mouth the Lord Jesus, and shalt believe in thine heart that God hath raised him from the dead, thou shalt be saved" (Rom. 10:9). Do this before you look for spiritual gifts, because if you are not yet in the Body, you do not have a spiritual gift at all.

Second, you have to believe in spiritual gifts. Most Christians who don't believe in spiritual gifts are that way because they haven't been told. In my long experience I do not think I can recall any Christian who has listened to teaching on spiritual gifts and not come out a believer. But the fact of the matter is that despite the books and seminars and sermons and seminary courses now available for Christian people, probably the majority of American Christians still have a minimal knowledge of spiritual gifts. In most cases it is not their fault. I get shivers down my spine when I read James 3:1, "My brethren, be not many [teachers], knowing that we shall receive the greater [judgment]." This is so uncomfortable because it shifts the blame for ignorance of spiritual gifts on those of us who are responsible to teach the Word of God to others. It's not that the doctrine of spiritual gifts is some obscure or vague New Testament teaching like baptizing for the dead or the time of the rapture.

This is a question of faith. You must believe that God has given you a spiritual gift before you start the process of discovering it. I wrote chapter 1 to try to convince all Christians who read this book that they do have spiritual gifts. If I have failed in your case, the five steps in this chapter are not for you. For them to work there must be a sense of thankfulness to God that He has given you a gift, and a sense of joyful anticipation in finding out what it is.

Third, you have to be willing to work. The five steps I am about to suggest constitute a spiritual exercise. It is something that needs God's help to accomplish. God has given you one or more spiritual gifts for a reason. There is a job He wants you to do in the Body of Christ, a specific job that He has equipped you for. God knows whether you are serious about working for Him. If He sees that you just want to discover your gift for kicks or because it's the "in" thing to do, you cannot expect Him to help you do it.

If, however, you promise to use your spiritual gift for the glory of God and for the welfare of the Body of Christ, He will help you. Recognize the fact that this is God's best for you. Be open to what He wants to do through you. Discovering gifts is not an ego trip, although it will help your self-esteem tremendously. If you are ready for a life in the future as an active, productive Christian, you are ready for the five steps.

Fourth you have to pray. Before, during and after this process you have to pray. "If any of you lack wisdom," James says, "let him ask of God, that giveth to all men liberally" (Jas. 1:5). Beseech God sincerely and earnestly for His guidance all the way through the five steps.

Since He wants you to discover your spiritual gift, He certainly will give you all the help you need. Just ask and believe that He will. He will unlock the beautiful possibilities for a fruitful spiritual ministry that He has already placed within you.

With these four prerequisites, we are ready for the five steps necessary to discover your spiritual gift.

Step 1: Explore the Possibilities

The first step in planning many human endeavors is to lay out all the possible options. If you want to travel from Dallas to Philadelphia, for example, you need to know that it can be done by train, airplane, automobile, motorcycle, horseback, hitchhiking, bus, and other ways. If you choose to drive, you get out a map and explore the different possibilities for routes. This is normal and logical.

It is difficult to discover a spiritual gift if you do not know approximately what to look for ahead of time. The purpose of this first step, exploring the possibilities, is to become familiar enough with the gifts that God has given to the Body of Christ so that when you discover yours later on, you will recognize it for what it is.

As I see it, there are five ways to approach this exciting first step.

First, study the Bible. Naturally, the basic source of data about the possible spiritual gifts is in the Bible. Read the major passages on spiritual gifts time and again. Read them in several different versions. Find examples in the lives of good people in the Bible as to how these gifts might have worked in practice. Using whatever helps are available, cross-check Scripture references until you feel you are familiar with what is there.

Second, learn your church's position on gifts. As I have mentioned several times already, by no means is there universal agreement between churches and denominations as to which gifts are in operation today. Nor would I expect that these differences will be resolved in our entire generation.

But in the meanwhile, we have a generation of lost men and women who need to be won to Jesus Christ. We would be stupid to say that we will wait until we all agree on spiritual gifts and then we will start evangelizing the world. The church-growth point of view would say, let's go to it and evangelize the world with the equipment God has given to us now. If the next generation will have other equipment or more consensus on one thing or another, that is of minor concern to us now.

There is a high degree of probability that God is pleased with a variety of different gift-mixes among the churches and denominations. We are the way we are largely because God made us that way. He gives some of His servants two talents and some five, but He expects us to use all of them to accomplish the Master's purpose.

Because I believe strongly in commitment to the Body of Christ, I believe that when a Christian voluntarily belongs to a church, he or she ought to be under the discipline and authority of that church. On the matter of spiritual gifts, the major difference today usually surfaces over what we have referred to as the "sign gifts" mainly speaking in tongues, but others as well. Some churches expect the gift of tongues to be used in their worship services. Some have special services on Thursday or Saturday when tongues are used, but they do not allow it on Sunday morning. Some have no meetings in the church at all where tongues are used, but they do not object to it in house meetings or the private use of tongues in prayer. Other churches are convinced that tongues should not be used at all in our day and age.

When you find out what is the position of your church on this and other gifts, I suggest one of two courses of action. Either decide to be loyal to your church and its belief and practice or respectfully leave and ask God to take you to another church where you will feel more at home.

Notice, the thing I do not recommend is that you decide to stay where you are and try to convince the church or certain individuals in it that they should change their position. The energy that such activity saps from the church is enormous. Many churches have gone through bitter splits over this issue because it has been allowed to fester under the surface until it could no longer be controlled. God did not give spiritual gifts for dissension and hard feelings. He gave spiritual gifts to enhance the health and vitality and growth of the Body. Every unit of spiritual energy being used to fight battles over spiritual gifts is one unit that cannot be used for reaching out to lost men and women. I believe that God prefers our energies to be used in seeing that the lost are found and that the church grows.

As a church member you have a right to know where your particular church stands on spiritual gifts. When you learn what it is, you will then have better parameters within which to explore possibilities.

Third, read extensively. Never before has there been a richer literary fare on spiritual gifts for Christian readers. In this book you will find my opinion on 27 of the gifts, but it is by no means the last word. Read the 10 books I recommend in the introduction. List the points where they agree on the definition of a particular gift and where they disagree. Put all that together with what you are learning from the Bible and make up your own mind. What difference does it really make if what I think is the gift of prophecy someone else thinks is the word of knowledge? God is overseeing the whole thing, and He is probably more broad-minded and more understanding than most of us give Him credit for. In most cases He can use us for His glory the way we are.

Fourth, get to know gifted people. Seek out and talk to Christian people who have discovered, developed and are using their spiritual gift or gifts. Find out how they articulate what their gifts are and how they interpret their ministry through gifts.

Fifth, make gifts a conversation piece. Contemporary Christians have come a long way in understanding spiritual gifts, but even so, a large number are still reluctant to talk about them to each other with ease. There is somewhat of an attitude that "If I talk about my spiritual gift people will think I am bragging," or, "If I talk about not having a gift it is a cop-out." I hope that soon we will shed our inhibitions and will be able to share openly with each other what our gifts are or what they are not. This will help us, our friends, and our children to know what the possibilities for gifts are.

Step 2: Experiment with as Many as You Can

Ray Stedman says, "You discover a spiritual gift just like you discovered your natural talents!"[1]

You would never know you had a talent for bowling, for example, if you hadn't tried it. You would never know you could write poetry if you had never tried. I wonder if I have a talent for hang-gliding? But I will never know unless I try it.

Obviously there are some spiritual gifts on the list that do not lend themselves easily to experiment. I do not know how to suggest an experiment with the gift of miracles or martyrdom, for example. I hope I myself never have to experiment with the gift of exorcism. But, while some gifts are like that, the majority are not. You can experiment with them, and I recommend that you do so as much as possible.

One starting point is to look around and see what needs you can identify. Then try to do something to meet a need. Look for the needs of other people. Look for the needs of the church. Find out where you can be useful in any way, and do it.

Be available for any job around the church you might be asked to do. When you get an assignment, undertake it in prayer. Ask the Lord to show you through that experience whether you might have a spiritual gift along those lines. Hang in there and work hard. Discovering gifts does not usually come easily. Give each job a fair shake and do not give up easily.

While you are experimenting with the gifts it is just as important to answer the question: "Which gifts don't I have?" as the opposite question: "Which gifts do I have?" Every gift you find you do not have reduces the number of options you need to work with for getting the positive answer.

When I graduated from Fuller Seminary back in the mid-fifties, I had learned next to nothing about spiritual gifts. I think that evangelical leaders by and large were still spooked out by the Pentecostal movement at that time and had not yet articulated their position on the gifts. We certainly were not taught that we had gifts and needed to discover, develop and use them in those days. After seminary I was ordained by an evangelical, Bible-believing church, but not one of the seven ministers on my ordaining council asked me if I had spiritual gifts or knew what they were. I was accepted and served under two evangelical mission agencies. Neither one asked questions about spiritual gifts on their application forms. So, I went to Bolivia in 1956 ignorant of spiritual gifts.

However, even though I didn't know much about

spiritual gifts, I did know what I was going to be. Those were the days when Billy Graham had moved into orbit. He became the hero of many seminary students including myself. I marveled at the way he would preach to a stadium full of people, deliver a simple Bible message, give an invitation, and see people get up all over the place, fill the aisles, and pour down front to make a decision for Christ. That was for me! My friends and I would imitate Billy Graham's gestures in our preaching classes. We would try to preach with a North Carolina accent. We learned to articulate "The Bible says . . . " with appropriate sparks of fire in our eyes.

By the time I was ready to go to the mission field, I had it all figured out. Billy Graham could have America —I was going to take Bolivia! In my mind I could see thousands and thousands of Bolivians finding Christ through my messages.

I had to spend some time learning Spanish, of course, but when I did, I was ready to go. I prepared a beautiful sermon in Spanish and used all the homiletical skills I had learned in seminary. I thought the sermon even had one or two things in it that Billy Graham himself might not have thought of. Then I preached the sermon with all my heart and gave the invitation. Nobody came!

Disappointed and somewhat dejected, I tried to figure out what had happened. Perhaps it had to do with prayer. Even at best I have never been a great prayer warrior, but with all the effort it took me to prepare the sermon that time, I had to admit that I had hardly prayed at all. So I made up another sermon with symmetrical design and sound doctrine. But this time I prayed intensely before I went into the pulpit. The results were the same. People acted as if they were permanently glued to their seats.

I then thought that something in my life must be

blocking my relationship with the Lord. The consecration theology I was taught had programmed me to feel that I must not properly be "presenting my body a living sacrifice," for if I were doing that, certainly God would bless my evangelistic ministry.

My thoughts went back to seminary again. I recalled a professor of personal evangelism who used to keep our class spellbound with stories of how God had used him to win others to Christ. He would tell of how he would get on a bus, sit next to a total stranger, and by the time they got off the bus the stranger would have accepted Christ. I was impressed!

So I got on a bus and took a seat next to a total stranger. By the time we got off the bus he was mad at me! I was devastated.

For months and even years during that first term of missionary service I went through experience after experience like that. I wanted to be Bolivia's Billy Graham, but something was preventing me from doing it.

Then little by little I began to learn about spiritual gifts. A close missionary friend of mine, Kenneth Decker, of the New Testament Missionary Union, got me reading Alex Hay's book, *The New Testament Order for Church and Missionary*. As I studied the book and the Scripture references it suggested, and as I shared with Kenneth Decker, the biblical teaching on gifts came into focus. And then one day I made what I consider the most important spiritual discovery of my Christian life —God had not given me the gift of evangelist!

From that day on, I have been a better Christian, a better missionary, a more joyous person, a better husband and father, and a more competent servant of God. To go back to Swindoll's fable, I was no longer an eagle trying to learn to climb a tree. When I realized the fact that in the day of judgment, God is not going to hold me accountable for what I did as an evangelist I felt liberated. Guilt rolled off like the pack on the back of Christian in *Pilgrim's Progress*. It was God Himself who had not wanted me to be the Billy Graham of Bolivia. What a relief!

I had experimented with a spiritual gift. I had tried hard to use it. And I had come to the very important discovery that I did not have the gift.

Let me hasten to say that, while I do not have the gift of evangelist, like every other Christian I do have a role of witness. Wherever I go and at all times I try to be a good representative of God. I know how to share Christ, and I occasionally lead a person to the Lord. Not having the gift of evangelist should never be a cop-out from consistent witnessing.

Step 3: Examine Your Feelings

Somewhere along the line, personal feelings have fallen into disrepute with many evangelicals. If a Christian is found enjoying life, according to them something must be wrong. But things are changing. The new teaching on spiritual gifts is opening the way for an age in which serving God can be fun. I appreciate Ray Stedman for telling it like it is when he says, "Somewhere the idea has found deep entrenchment in Christian circles that doing what God wants you to do is always unpleasant; that Christians must always make choices between doing what they want to do and being happy and doing what God wants them to do and being completely miserable."[2] And Kenneth Kinghorn takes aim at the right target when he observes that "maturing Christians grow beyond shallow concepts of discipleship that equate unhappiness with serving God."[3]

My concept is this. It is the same God who gives spiritual gifts who also oversees the way each one of us is made up in our total being. God knows every detail of our psychological condition, our glands and hormones, our metabolism, our total personality. He understands our feelings perfectly. And He knows that if we enjoy doing a task we do a better job at it than if we do not enjoy it. So part of the plan of God, as I understand it, is to match the spiritual gift He gives us with our feelings in such a way that if we really have a gift we will feel good using it. This may well be why, as we saw in chapter 1, God reserves the assigning of spiritual gifts to Himself. All the computers in IBM wouldn't be equipped to do that for the hundreds of millions of Christians around the world, but it is no problem to God Almighty.

It seems like there is also good biblical teaching that this is the way God wants to lead His people. Psalm 37:4 says, "Delight thyself also in the Lord; and he shall give thee the desires of thine heart." Then Philippians 2:13 adds, "For it is God which worketh in you both to will and to do of his good pleasure." Apparently, when a Christian is doing God's will, he will be doing what he wants to do. Biblically, then, it seems that there is no conflict between enjoying yourself and pleasing God.

Findley Edge says that a Christian who finds God's calling through his or her gift will get a "eureka feeling." That means that the person says, "This, really, is what I had rather do for God than anything else in the world."[4]

Edge points out that when a person exercises a ministry, that individual, like it or not, subconsciously communicates the motivation behind the ministry. If it is negative, those who receive the ministry get a negative message and the total effect is less than ideal. If it is a positive motivation that comes across, the ministry is thereby enhanced and made more effective.

During that same first term as a missionary, I also discovered, largely through feelings, that I did not have the gift of pastor.

We were assigned by our mission to the small village of San Jose de Chiquitos where, among other things, we were to plant a new church. We started the church, small and struggling as it was. But in the course of trying out pastoral work I learned that I was not well-equipped to handle people's personal problems. When someone begins to tell me about his or her personal life, I come unglued. I tend to worry about it, lose sleep over it, want to cry, and overreact in many ways. I make all the wrong moves. I cannot trust my intuitions. In a word, my feelings tell me that God has not given me the gift.

Of course I do have a role of occasionally helping others through their problems and relating in a pastoral way when certain situations come up. Members of my family, certain friends, and at times students need my help and I try to give it to them as best I can. My rate of success at personal counseling is extremely low, if not zero. And because I react so poorly I tend to avoid counseling situations as much as possible. It is hard for some others to understand what a drain on emotional energies listening to other people's problems can be on those of us who don't have the gift.

Once I did accept a pastorate even when I knew I didn't have the gift. There was an important principle behind it, which Findley Edge expresses well when he says, "There are times when we must engage in action simply on the basis of 'ought.' A particular job needs to be done and a sense of 'ought' is the best (or only) motivation we have for doing it."[5] In my case the "ought" was filling in as pastor of a large city church in Bolivia during the time the pastor, Jaime Rios, was on leave of absence to coordinate the massive nationwide

Evangelism-in-Depth effort in 1965. Bolivia needed to be evangelized more strenuously and, because I believed so strongly in that goal, I was willing to do what I was called upon to do, even though it meant ministering for a time on the basis of a role rather than a gift.

While feelings may have to be put aside from time to time on the basis of an "ought" situation, that should only be temporary. The normal thing is that Christians should feel turned on to the work they are doing for God because they have discovered the spiritual gift that God has given them. While experimenting with the gifts, then, it is important to examine your feelings.

Step 4: Evaluate Your Effectiveness

Since the spiritual gifts are task-oriented it is not out of order to expect them to work. If God has given you a gift, He has done so because He wants you to accomplish something for Him in the context of the Body of Christ. Gifted people get results. Postulating that God wants us to be successful is not contradictory to sincere Christian humility. If you experiment with a gift and consistently find that what it is supposed to do doesn't happen, you probably have discovered another one of the gifts that God has not given you.

This is where I got my first clue that I do not have the gift of evangelist. I tried with dedication and sincerity and it didn't work. I tried public evangelism and bombed. I tried personal evangelism and got knots in my stomach and tongue-tied. When I observed some of my friends who were effortlessly witnessing and leading large numbers of people to Christ, I then knew that compared to them I was getting very little supernatural help in evangelizing. God was trying to tell me something.

If you have the gift of evangelist, people will come to

Christ regularly through your ministry. If you have the gift of exhortation you will help people through their problems and see lives straightened out. If you have the gift of healing, sick people will get well. If you have the gift of administration, the organization will run smoothly. When true gifts are in operation, whatever is supposed to happen will happen.

Gift 3: The Gift of Teaching

During our first term on the mission field not only did I discover that I did not have the gifts of evangelist and pastor, but I also discovered a gift that I did have: the gift of teaching.

I now have become very conscious of the fact that when I get to the final judgment, God is going to ask me tough questions about what I did with the gift of teaching. Since I know the question is coming, I make it a point to do everything I can to have a satisfactory answer ready.

The gift of teaching is the special ability that God gives to certain members of the Body of Christ to communicate information relevant to the health and ministry of the Body and its members in such a way that others will learn.

It will be seen immediately that this definition has effectiveness built in: "Others will learn." It is always necessary to keep in mind what teaching is for. Michael Griffiths says, "Traditionally too much Christian teaching is pulpit soliloquy and nobody ever checks up to see whether anybody takes notice or whether teaching produces any action."[6] How true!

Because I have the gift of teaching, I fully expect people to learn, both in my classes and through my writings. If I thought that I would get any other kind of results, I would doubt that I had the gift. I do not believe

I am thinking more highly of myself than I ought to think. I believe I am thinking soberly. I frequently get letters from students that say, "Your course was the best learning experience I have had since leaving seminary 20 years ago," or words to that effect. Frankly, I expect that to happen just as Billy Graham expects people to get up and come forward when he gives an evangelistic invitation. But I still love to get the letters.

That doesn't mean I never bomb. Unfortunately, I do. A few months ago, for example, I was invited to conduct a seminar on church growth and found out only after I arrived that many of those who had signed up were neither born-again Christians nor did they believe that fulfilling the Great Commission to make disciples of all nations was very important. By the end of the week both they and I were anxious to go home, and the evaluations that came in afterward were dismal. This is the exception, however. On a scale of 1-10, my ratings usually come out between 8 and 10, although in almost every class there are some I rub the wrong way and they give me a 2 or 3.

The gift of teaching is mentioned in all three of the primary lists of spiritual gifts: Romans 12, 1 Corinthians 12 and Ephesians 4. This does not mean it is any more valid than a gift mentioned only once, but it probably does mean that it is more universal. While it is true that different churches have different gift-mixes, I think that virtually every church would receive the gift of teacher as a part of its mix. I also think that the percentage of members of the Body of Christ who receive the gift of teacher would turn out to be higher than the percentage for many other gifts. This remains to be researched.

The gift of teaching comes in many, many varieties. Some people have a gift of teaching that enables them to communicate well to children. My gift is basically for adults and, frankly, kids think I'm a terrible bore. I make it a practice never to accept teaching invitations for college age or under. Some with the gift of teaching are good at one-on-one teaching such as Paul with Timothy, or Aquila and Priscilla with Apollos (see Acts 18:26). I do a good bit of that as a mentor for theses and dissertations, but I have found that (a) I don't enjoy it and (b) there are many others on our faculty who do a far superior job compared to me. My strength is standing before a classroom with 30 or 40 people. Beyond that my effectiveness falls off. I could never match the kind of teaching Bill Gothard does, for example, holding the attention of 10 or 15 thousand people at once through an intensive seminar.

Some use their gift of teaching through media such as radio or television. Some are good at teaching laypeople, some are good at teaching professionals. Some are able to use their gift of teaching through writing, other teachers find writing a drag and do as little of it as possible. Some teach through the medium of preaching, some through music, some through drama.

Teaching is usually a full-time gift. Unlike other gifts that are used only occasionally like exorcism or discerning of spirits, and unlike celibacy which is relatively passive once it's discovered and in operation, teaching usually implies a steady, regular use with lots of time in study and preparation. Not only does that apply to professional teachers such as myself, but also to lay Sunday School teachers in the church. If a Sunday School teacher has the gift of teaching, he or she will probably not be able to do very much more as far as service to the church is concerned. Those with the gift, love to spend large amounts of time studying the lesson. They work hard with details, they organize and reorganize. They search for illustrations that will make the material more meaningful. They spend time on visuals. For example, I find myself sometimes spending two or three hours working on an overhead projection slide which I will use for perhaps 15 to 30 seconds in a class. But if it nails down a point effectively, it is well worth it and it brings me tremendous satisfaction.

Teachers who have the gift are patient with their students. They create an atmosphere in their classes where students feel free to raise questions of any kind without feeling that they will be put down or made to look stupid before the others. Teachers have a fear of projecting any attitude that could be interpreted as manipulation or humiliation. They are not threatened or defensive when criticism comes. Such attitudes and intuitions are not the kind of thing that can be learned by just anyone. They are part of the supernatural dimension of having a spiritual gift.

Several possible combinations come to mind when we think of teacher as part of a hyphenated gift. The Bible itself mentions pastor-teacher (see Eph. 4:11) as a frequent combination. Another is preacher-teacher. Not all preachers have (or need) the gift of teaching, but some do. Prophet-teacher seems to be a combination we find often in the New Testament. I would surmise that such a combination was more necessary in the first century or two, before the New Testament had been compiled and was circulating among the churches, than it is today, at least among more literate societies. Perhaps among Christian peoples today who are largely illiterate prophet-teacher would be found more frequently, and the experience of African independent churches seems to bear this out.

One other frequent hyphenated combination is scholar-teacher, a combination I myself have. My hypothesis is that the "scholar" side is a contemporary way of expressing the gift of knowledge. Thus, in order properly to exercise my particular gift, I have to spend more time in research and study than others who may have the gift of teaching but who do not have it combined with the gift of knowledge.

How did I discover that I was a scholar-teacher? I first found out they were biblical options, I experimented with them, I enjoyed them a great deal, I found I was effective in doing them, and, one more thing: the gifts were confirmed by other members of the Body. This is step five.

Step 5: Expect Confirmation from the Body

If you think you have a spiritual gift and are trying to exercise it, but no one else in your church thinks you have it—you probably don't. It needs to be confirmed.

At this point you might find a conflict between Step 3 concerning your feelings and Step 5 concerning confirmation. Feelings are important, but they are far from infallible. You may have a deep desire to help other people, for example. You may feel strongly that God is calling you to minister through counseling or the gift of exhortation. But if you are experimenting with counseling and find over a period of time no one seeks you out for help or recommends their friends and relatives to you or writes you notes telling how much you have helped them, you have good reason to doubt the validity of your feelings as far as a spiritual gift is concerned. Confirmation from the Body is a check on all the steps. It is number 5 in order, but in many ways it is the most important of all.

The gifts, according to our working definition, are given for use within the context of the Body. It is necessary, then, that the other members of the Body have the final word in confirming your gift.

One of the reasons confirmation from the Body is so important is that it builds in a system of accountability for the use of your gift. Whereas it's true that we are ultimately accountable to God, more immediately we are accountable to each other and we need to take this seriously. The depth of commitment that this brings with it is vividly described by Elizabeth O'Connor. She points out that accountability is never comfortable. She says, "Commitment at the point of my gifts means that I must give up being a straddler . . . . Life will not be the smorgasbord I have made it, sampling and tasting here and there."[7]

If you have the gift of administration or helps or evangelist or mercy, but nobody else knows it, you may choose to be lazy about using it and no one will know the difference. But once it is known and confirmed by the Body, your friends will expect to see it in action. That's why I pointed out earlier that a desire to work hard is a prerequisite for discovering spiritual gifts. When members of the Body confirm one anothers' gifts, more gets done just on the basis of people working harder.

For some years I thought I had the gift of administration. Somewhat against my will at first, I was talked into taking over the administration of the mission agency we were serving under. As I experimented with administration, I began to enjoy it quite a bit, so far as feelings were concerned, it seemed like it might be a gift. Then when my position came up for confirmation at the field conference meeting there was a good bit of disagreement among fellow workers as to my appointment and whenever a vote came I would barely squeak by. I needed someone with the gift of exhortation to tell me to get out of administration and go back to teaching, but either that person wasn't there or I was not listening. So I continued for some years and predictably the mission did not advance greatly under my leadership.

Only after I got back to the United States and read a book, *The Making of a Christian Leader*, by a close friend of mine, Ted Engstrom, did I understand clearly that I never did have the gift of administration. In this case, another member of the Body confirmed to me that I did not have the gift, and I have been grateful to Ted Engstrom ever since.

How You Can Find Yours

This chapter has been so autobiographical that an explanation might be proper. As many evangelists have discovered, personal testimonies can be extremely helpful in motivating people, because they provide something of flesh and blood to identify with. Abstract concepts are fine, but they rarely move people. My purpose in this chapter has been to help you see more clearly how you can begin the exciting process of discovering your spiritual gift or gifts.

Although, as I said in the beginning, this approach will not help everybody, I am quite confident it will help some. Let me illustrate how it can work by quoting a letter from one of the most successful church growth pastors in the United Methodist Church, Joe Harding. Pastor Harding's church, the Central United Protestant Church of Richland, Washington is one of the largest and fastest growing churches of the Northwest, an area not particularly known for explosive church growth. Joe Harding had enrolled in a Doctor of Ministry church growth seminar that I was teaching in the Eastern Washington Fuller extension center with classes meeting in his church facilities. A few days after the lecture on spiritual gifts and church growth, he wrote this letter:

Your class was particularly helpful to me in making

a major decision. Just a few days before the class I had received a telephone call from one of our denominational executives asking me to move to a national office in the Board of Discipleship in Nashville to head up a new program of evangelism. I was told that I was their first choice and they really wanted me to accept this responsibility. I am acquainted with the program and I am enthusiastic about it.

However, as I weighed the matter very carefully it was clear to me that my gifts are not primarily in administration, but in preaching and teaching and in pastoring. When I measured my personal gifts against the requirements of this challenging job, it was very easy for me to decline and to feel that God was calling me to remain in this congregation to demonstrate the potential of dynamic and vital growth within the Methodist church.

I was in agony when I first received the call, because I felt I could not decline such a challenging opportunity. Your emphasis on the joy that you find in exercising the gifts put the matter in an entirely different perspective. I find that tremendous joy in standing before the congregation that I preach to, Sunday after Sunday. I simply know that that is what God is calling me to do.

So your class came at a most appropriate time in my life and I simply want to share my gratitude with you.

The thrill I got from receiving Joe Harding's letter could not have been any less than that which Billy Graham must feel when 3,000 people come forward in one of his crusades. I now thank God that I am not the Billy Graham of Bolivia as I once thought I would be. God had something much better—for *me.* He has a similar exciting and fulfilling thing in mind for *you*.

A sequel to the above story that may have far-reaching effects for future church growth within the United Methodist Church is that the man who ultimately did fill the position in Nashville, Dr. George Hunter, III, does have that special gift-mix that Joe Harding knew he didn't have. Hunter is not a quiet, low-key pastoral type who could be fulfilled preaching to the same congregation Sunday after Sunday. He is an aggressive, hard-headed, fast-moving type of leader who can lead a program of evangelism and church growth forward without being daunted by the forces of opposition that are still making their voices heard within that denomination. It has come about because God is the one who distributes the gifts, and in this case both the individuals concerned and the Body as a whole were in tune with what God was trying to do.

As you and your particular part of the Body of Christ do a similar thing, power for church growth that may now be hidden or dormant will be awakened for the glory of God. It works because it is God's design.

Notes

1. Ray C. Stedman, *Body Life* (Glendale: Regal Books, 1972), p. 54.
2. *Ibid.*
3. Kenneth Cain Kinghorn, *Gifts of the Spirit* (Nashville: Abingdon Press, 1976), p. 110.
4. Findley B. Edge, *The Greening of the Church* (Waco: Word Books, 1971), p. 141.
5. *Ibid.*, p. 142.
6. Michael Griffiths, *Cinderella's Bethrothal Gifts*, (Robesonia, PA: OMF Books, 1978), p. 36.
7. Elizabeth O'Connor, *Eighth Day of Creation* (Waco: Word Books, 1971), pp. 42,43.

5.
The Pastor and His Gift-Mix

Up to this point my treatment of spiritual gifts has been somewhat general. The groundwork needed to be laid. It is impossible to be specific about spiritual gifts and how they relate to church growth unless the fog of ignorance about spiritual gifts is dispelled. From time to time I mentioned certain ways that spiritual gifts relate to the growth of the church, but the stress has been on the general health of Christian individuals and churches. Of course it is necessary that the church as a whole be healthy if it is to grow well, but in many cases churches are not growing because they experience a special problem concerning the operation of spiritual gifts.

The Pastor Is Still the Key

The place to begin to probe some of these problems is with the pastor. As far as the growth of the local church is concerned (the spread of the gospel on new ground will be discussed in chapter 7), the pastor is the key individual. The pastor, of course, is not the only factor for growth in a local church, but he is probably the most important one.

In my book, *Your Church Can Grow*, I described seven vital signs of a healthy church, and named the pastor as the first vital sign. As I did, I wondered how the hypothesis would hold up under the scrutiny of other professionals in the field. Feedback over the past two years has caused me to modify some of my postulations on other of the vital signs, but if anything the hypothesis as to the pastor's being the key individual for growth in the local church has been strengthened.

Since that book was written, very significant studies have been published on the growth trends of three of our major mainline denominations, the United Methodist Church, the United Presbyterian Church and the Southern Baptist Convention. They all verified the crucial role of the pastor.

The Methodist study, for example, speaks of the several organizations now studying church growth: "In one way or another, they all recognize the pastor is the key person. They may disagree about how the pastor should be involved, but they all agree that the pastor must be involved." There are many reasons for this, but the study highlights one of them by arguing that "the pastor's involvement signals his or her commitment to the conviction that one of the most important tasks of the local congregation is that of extending the ministry of the church to include more persons."[1]

The United Presbyterian study, after analyzing causes of decline and growth, set forth 10 "implications for positive action" that the authors felt the United Presbyterian Church must take if it is to reverse the general downward trend of church membership. The first dealt with motivation (the church must affirm that it expects growth), but the second had to do with the pastor. It argued that "The United Presbyterian Church must adequately recognize strong pastoral competence as a decisive factor for the vitality and outreach of a congregation." It mentioned that all their formal and informal research led to the same conclusion, namely, that "pastoral leadership is crucial to almost all aspects of vital congregational life, and certainly to membership growth."[2] When they compared the perceptions of members of growing churches to members of declining churches, they found that pastors of growing churches were seen to be taking more responsibility for church growth, having more influence on what happens in the church, promoting a sense of unity, and more able to handle conflict.

The most comprehensive test of the "seven vital signs" was conducted by the Home Mission Board of the Southern Baptist Convention in 1977. They designed and carried out a computerized study of 30,029 Southern Baptist churches to find out which were the 425 fastest growing in the denomination. A special study was made of these, seeing if the vital signs fit. In-depth case studies were then carried out in the 15 churches that showed the best growth records to compare them to the general data. As to the first vital sign, the pastor, the report states, "Pastors of the top 15 fastest growing churches agree the key is leadership .... While giving credit to others, all say they are responsible to God for the growth, nurture, direction, outreach and ministry of the church. They feel they are God's man in God's church in God's time."[3]

Between 1976 and 1978 the Hartford Seminary Foundation gathered a top-level research team of sociologists of religion, church planners and denominational executives to study why mainline denominations in the United States have been declining since 1965. One of their conclusions is that "both wisdom and the available hard data clearly converge to tell us that the role of pastor is critical for 'growing' a congregation." Then the report significantly adds, "Unfortunately they are less clear in telling us specifically what it is about that role or about the qualities of the person filling that role that is most important."[4]

That is precisely one of the purposes of this chapter. I do not have all the answers, but I think I can at least make a start in describing some of the qualities a church-growth pastor must have by putting them in the context of spiritual gifts. As time goes by, these ideas can be tested and later adjusted if necessary in the light of new feedback. I hope that within the fairly near future we begin to get handles on just what equipment a pastor does need to lead a growing church, and then hopefully adjust our systems of ministerial training, whether Bible schools or seminaries, to focus on those particular needs.

It is understandable why some pastors react negatively to the hypothesis that they are the key person for growth in their churches. While some resistance to this may be due to humility, probably much more is due to a reluctance on the part of many pastors to shoulder so much responsibility. In neither case are the objections adequate. Church people in general are coming to realize more than ever before that if a person accepts the responsibility of being the pastor of a church, he accepts the primary responsibility for its growth or decline just as much as an airplane pilot accepts responsibility for keeping his plane in the air. It won't fly without wings and stabilizer and engine, true. But recognizing that doesn't change the fact that the pilot is the one who makes it fly.

It is true theologically that Jesus is the Head of the church. But He also chooses and equips His under-shepherds. In a church structure there may be 100 or 500 or 5,000 members, but one person above all others in that church is most directly answerable to Jesus Christ, the head of the universal church, for the welfare of the particular local body he is responsible for. That person is the pastor.

This is why pastoral gift-mixes are so crucial for church growth. Given the right person with the right gift-mix, virtually any church has great possibilities for growth.

The Myth of the "Omnicompetent" Pastor

There is an outmoded view of the pastor's role which, although diminishing, strongly persists in some circles today. It is the view that the pastor is hired by the congregation to do all the work of the church. The better the pastor, the more the people of the church can relax and become spectators. It is not only an outmoded view, it is also unbiblical.

The Bible's view of the Body of Christ is that it is an organism with all the members functioning together. The best pastor is not one who relieves members of their responsibilities, but one who makes sure each member has a responsibility and is working hard at it.

The pastor is one of many members of the Body. He is not the Head (that is reserved for Jesus) but he may be something like the nervous system which carries messages from the head to the various members of the body and makes sure the members are working together in harmony. The smooth coordination of the body uniquely depends on him. Many church members do not recognize or accept this. While they may not expect the pastor to do everything, they expect him to do most things. The stereotype that many church people have of pastors is that they need to be accomplished public speakers, skilled counselors, biblical and theological scholars, public relations experts, administrators, social ethicists, masters of ceremony, soul winners, stimulating teachers, funeral directors and competent at everything else except perhaps at walking on water. This "omnicompetent" pastor is the person that hundreds of pulpit committees are searching for.

Of course, they never find him. Anyone at all coversant with spiritual gifts could predict this. No one in the Body has all the gifts, pastors included. When this simple fact is overlooked, though, disappointment is right around the corner. Such disappointment is not really necessary. It can be significantly reduced if and when pastoral responsibility is evaluated and job descriptions are written on the basis of spiritual gifts.

If this is the case, what spiritual gifts are necessary for a successful, church-growth pastor?

It might be best to approach this question first of all from the negative point of view. What gifts are *not* necessary for the pastor of a growing church? My suggestion is that only two of the gifts are indispensable for the pastor of a rapidly growing church. That leaves 25 which are, shall we say, optional. There is no need discussing all 25. However, four of them in particular deserve mention because they are four qualities which many people mistakenly think a church-growth pastor needs. I refer to the gifts of pastor, exhortation, evangelist and administration.

Gift 20: The Gift of Pastor

Up to this point, I have been using the word "pastor"

in its broad, contemporary sense. In current vocabulary it signifies the person who is the designated head of a local church. He is also called the minister, the rector, the parson, or sometimes the preacher. Now, as far as the gift is concerned, we need to use "pastor" in a more technical sense.

It strikes some people as odd when they first hear that a successful pastor does not need the pastoral gift. In fact, very few senior ministers of large, growing churches do have the gift of pastor. Almost by definition, if they had the gift they wouldn't be where they are. And those who do head up large churches and still have a pastoral gift frequently find it a source of frustration. If not properly handled and understood, the gift often becomes a cause of non-growth as we will see shortly.

But, first, what is the pastoral gift? *The gift of pastor is the special ability that God gives to certain members of the Body of Christ to assume a long-term personal responsibility for the spiritual welfare of a group of believers.*

The word "pastor" itself is borrowed from animal husbandry, particularly sheep raising. It is by no means as universally an understood vocation today as it was in first century Palestine, so it needs some explanation. The pastor of a group of Christians is the person responsible under Jesus, who is the Master Shepherd, for teaching, feeding, healing the wounds, developing unity, helping people find their gifts, and doing whatever else is necessary to see that they continue in the faith and grow in their spiritual lives.

Several biblical words are used as synonyms for pastor. The English words elder, presbyter, overseer, and bishop (sometimes interchanged depending on the translation) all mean pastor. Because these words are used in such a variety of ways in our contemporary churches, it is helpful to distinguish between the *office* of pastor and the *gift* of pastor. Most of those we call pastors in America are people occupying the *office* of pastor. They have a staff position in the church. The point I am making here is that not everyone who has the *office* of pastor needs the gift of pastor, and furthermore there are many men and women with the *gift* of pastor who do not have the *office* of pastor by being placed on a church staff.

In passing, note that "preaching" has not been listed as a spiritual gift. Perhaps it could be, but I do not feel it would be any more useful than adding "making movies" or "radio broadcasting" or "writing." All of these are forms of communications media that can be used for the exercise of any number of the more substantial gifts. Through preaching, for example, some exercise their gift of evangelist, some their gift of teaching, some their gift of faith, and others their gift of healing, and so forth. We often require good preaching as a quality for those we hire to occupy the office of pastor, and there is nothing wrong with that. But many if not most people with the gift of pastor will not be accomplished preachers. While preachers tend to draw the attention of others to themselves, pastors tend to pour out their attention on others.

Another thing. While the gift of pastor is frequently attached to teacher in the hyphenated pastor-teacher gift-mix as we saw in Ephesians 4:11, the two gifts can and do operate independently of each other. It is true that teaching is a part of the responsibility of one with the gift of pastor, but that can adequately be exercised through a Christian role rather than a special spiritual gift. Teaching can involve a short-term relationship between student and teacher and still be done well. Pastoring implies a much more patient and personal relationship over the long haul. No church hires a person to come in for a week to do pastoral work like they will hire an evangelist or a Bible teacher or a church-growth consultant. A teacher can have a low need for people, but a pastor typically has a high need for people. A teacher can be content-centered, motivation-centered or task-centered. A pastor usually is person-centered.

Now as soon as we understand that the gift of pastor is not necessarily what your senior minister has, a vast and exciting possibility is opened for lay-people to begin to exercise the gift of pastor. In many churches the gift is not seen among lay-people simply because no one has looked for it. It has been assumed that when a church hires a pastor and pays his salary, they are paying him to do the pastoral work for them. By doing so, they may unknowingly be throttling the growth of their church and not understand the reason why.

Church Growth and Pastoral Gifts

I believe that the gift of pastor is a universal gift. In other words, there is probably not a single local church which does not have the gift of pastor included in its gift-mix. This may not be true of some parachurch organizations, but it is necessarily true of churches. There is ample New Testament teaching on how pastors or elders were provided by God for every church. Paul saw that they were identified and properly ordained even in the very young churches that he started as a foreign missionary. Acts 14:23, for example, tells us that Paul and his fellow missionaries ordained elders in *every church.*

I further believe that the gift of pastor is given to both men and women. In some cultures God undoubtedly gives it to more women than men. In others God may give it to more men than women. As I have mentioned before, God is wonderfully flexible and He adapts the way He works in the world to each one of the thousands and thousands of cultures where the Word of God is known around the world.

How about our culture? I would suppose that in the contemporary Anglo-American culture, God will have distributed the gift of pastor about evenly between men and women. The proportion might be different for Hispanic-American culture or Korean-American culture or Black-American culture, or for any of the other fascinating pieces of the social mosaic that makes up present-day United States. I don't know. Here is another area where some good research would be invaluable.

Please let me say parenthetically that I am not intending to take a position on the ordination of women at this point. The topic is much too inflammatory to be discussed here, and it would be an unnecessary digression. I don't believe the pastoral gift needs to be certified by the formal process of ordination as usually defined by our ecclesiastical structures. But I certainly believe that in both men and women it needs to be discovered, confirmed by the Body, developed and used for the glory of God and the growth of the church.

With this, we are ready for the question: How many people in the Body, men and women, should we expect have been given the gift of pastor? And then: How does this gift relate directly to the growth or non-growth of churches?

Celebration-Congregation-Cell

It is helpful to think of the gift of pastor as essentially a congregational gift. Here I am using the word "congregation" in terms of the celebration-congregation-cell structure, which has been described as one of the seven vital signs of a healthy church.[5] The celebration, usually the Sunday morning worship service which brings together all those who belong to the membership circle of the church, is not limited in size except by secondary considerations. The congregation, which brings together people who belong to fellowship circles has an optimum size of between 40 and 120 members. The cell, where personal intimacy and accountability take place on a deeper level, should run between 8 and 12 persons. Cells take various forms. For example, in most Southern Baptist churches, Sunday School classes function as cells.

While the person with the *office* of pastor, or the senior minister, usually leads the celebration, he does not need a pastoral gift for that function. On the other side of the spectrum, the cell group, when operating properly, draws each of the members into a mutual caring dynamic which requires only the *role* of pastor on the part of each of the members, not necessarily the *gift*. The spiritual gift of pastor is not too relevant, then, to either the celebration or the cell.

However, it is in that intermediate structure, the congregation, where the pastoral gift becomes most relevant and finds its fullest expression. Churches that range from 100 to 250 members and seem to be having growth problems would do well to take a close look at this particular area of their church life. One of their problems might be that they have only one congregation when they need several, and that the requirements for pastoral care have already been stretched past the available resources.

What do I mean specifically?

A lay, part-time man or woman with the gift of pastor can usually handle from 8-15 families in their "flock" so to speak. The exact number depends on the degree of the gift they have, on the time available per week to use that gift, and on the cell or small group dynamic operating in the church. A professionally-trained, full-time minister who also has the gift of pastor can usually handle something between 50-100 families, depending again on the degree of gift and on the other responsibilities included in his job description.

Suppose that in a large church, then, you have a congregation of 100 members with 40 couples and 20 single adults. It may be an adult Bible class, a Sunday School department or a choir or a geographical grouping—all these and others are common structures for congregations. If it is a larger church, chances are that the members of this congregation will not have day-to-day access to the senior minister or to other staff members in a pastoral relationship. In my church of 3,200 members, for example, I have lunch with the senior minister about once a year and consider myself highly privileged, since there are only 365 days in a year when lunch is served. There is no way that he can or should be expected to pastor 3,200 people. Or even get to know them. Since he does not share Jerry Falwell's incredible ability to remember names, we help him out by wearing attractive name tags on our lapels for every service. The name tags have other functions as well, but they do save him some embarrassment.

How Many Have the Pastoral Gift?

In a situation like this, pastoral care on a congregational level, on a scale much smaller than the membership circle, becomes crucial. In our hypothetical congregation of 100 members, then, it would be reasonable to expect that God would have given the gift of pastor to about three or four members of that particular part of the Body of Christ. They would be lay, part-time men and women who would become responsible for the spiritual welfare of families in the congregation. They would be selected for this on the basis of spiritual gifts God has given them. They should also have some sort of formal, public recognition of that gift. If ordination is out of order, then some sort of commissioning or public consecration will suffice. But the point is that these gifts must be confirmed by the Body and set in action. God has already done His part by giving the gifts.

Now let's move from the larger church where the gift of pastor needs to be operative in the various sub-congregations to smaller churches where the membership group may be identical to the fellowship group. In other words, a one-congregation church. How is the growth of a church like this affected by the gift of pastor?

Here is Church A. It has 200 members and has been at that level for some years. The pastor of the church also happens to have the gift of pastor.

Here is Church B. It also has 200 members and has been plateaued. But in this case either the pastor does not have the gift of pastor, or he is part-time (as are, for example, 10,000 bivocational Southern Baptist pastors in America) and couldn't exercise his gift very much even if he did have it.

In Church A, because the pastor has the gift and loves to use it, he is likely to give a great deal of time to the members in visitation and meeting with groups and social activities. He is probably more people-oriented than task-oriented. He may emphasize "relational theology" in his messages. He may spend only a minimal time, if any, in working out growth goals for the church and planning as to how they can be implemented. In fact, he may not even want to do this because he is already worrying that with 200 members he is really doing an inadequate job of pastoring that many people. As we have said, even a full-time professional can handle only 50-100 families, and Church A has reached the upper limit.

If the pastor of Church A feels that he does not need any help in pastoring the flock, the chances are the church will not grow. No matter how much he may make public pronouncements about reaching the unchurched and winning souls, being relevant to the community and adding to the church membership, he unconsciously may make sure it does not happen. This has no malicious intent whatsoever. It grows out of a sincere desire to serve the Lord better with his gifts. That kind of a pastor would likely feel that he could do a better job of pastoring if the flock had fewer members, not more. So he cannot be expected to be enthusiastic about church growth.

How about church B? If the person hired as pastor is either part-time or doesn't have the gift of pastor and tries to do the pastoral work himself, the church will most likely decline over a period of two or three years. A minister without the gift of pastor can be expected to make every effort to arrange his schedule so he keeps busy in other good spiritual activities that take time and which leave him little time for pastoral work. He may prefer to prepare expository sermons rather than visit the hospital. He may give a great deal of time to administrative details and be available very little for counseling. He may feel more comfortable carrying his Christian witness to the world through civic organizations rather than spending much time with the fellowship groups in the church or in homes. If this is the case and the pastoral work thereby suffers, the health of the Body is damaged, and decline may be just around the corner.

But, in the final analysis, Church B actually has a

higher potential for growth than Church A. If it dawns on the pastor of Church B that God may have provided spiritual gifts to someone else in the congregation to do the pastoral work he tries to avoid, he would be elated. If, on the other hand, someone suggested this same thing to the pastor of Church A, he might feel threatened. Because of his spiritual gift, the pastor of Church A loves pastoral work and doesn't care to be freed to do something else. For Church B's pastor, just the opposite would happen. He would feel liberated. He could do what he likes to do and still keep his job.

Take heart, pastor without the gift of pastor! Your church has been given all the pastoral gifts it needs by the Lord Himself. But God is depending on you to see that the gifts are actuated. You have accepted the leadership of the church. In your church of 200 members you can assume that God has given the gift of pastor to around six or eight men and women whose Christian lives will be more abundantly fulfilled than ever when they are properly instructed and encouraged. They are waiting to be put to work. They will do a better job of caring for the sheep than you can, seminary degree and all. Get them involved and working. They'll be happier and more productive—and they'll love you for it.

Pastors and Cells

The hypothetical examples we have been using up to this point, with 12-15 families assigned to each man or woman with the pastoral gift, has presupposed a functioning cell or small group system in the church. In the cells pastoral care is taking place spontaneously without anyone necessarily having the gift of pastor. In such a case, the needs of church members for special pastoral care are lower than if cells are not operating. This means that when cells are doing part of the pastoral work, each person with the gift of pastor can be assigned more families.

Here is a rule of thumb: if something around 50 percent of the active church members are involved in cells, you should look for 3 to 4 percent of adult members with the gift of pastor. This gives them 12-15 families each. If, however, cell groups are not activated, more personal attention is required and each man or woman with the gift should be assigned only 8 to 10 families. Percentage-wise this figures to around 5 to 6 percent.

An example of how the latter is functioning at optimum level is Garden Grove Community Church. There Pastor Robert Schuller, like most other super-church pastors, does not have the gift of pastor. If he had a tendency to lose sleep over the personal spiritual welfare of his 9,000 plus members, he would long since have been put in a padded cell. He couldn't give his attention to dreaming big dreams, such as crystal cathedrals or television productions or 12 choirs or professional counseling services or new churches near Florida's Disneyworld. His pastoral role is even as likely to be used at the bedside of John Wayne or at Hubert Humphrey's funeral as with members of his own church.

But one reason why Garden Grove Community Church has enjoyed a steady pattern of growth over more than 20 years is that the members of the church do receive the pastoral care they need. At one time Garden Grove Community Church was a "Church B" kind of church, with 200 members and a pastor who did not have the spiritual gift of pastor. The only difference was that it did not plateau because Pastor Schuller understood that if he was not going to be able to give the necessary pastoral care to his church members, someone would have to do it for him. He organized a training program called the Lay Ministers Training Center, designed to help the members of his church discover their gifts such as evangelism, hospitality, teaching, pastor and others, and then put them to work. At the present time Garden Grove Community Church has 529 lay ministers of pastoral care attending to the pastoral work of the church under the general supervision of a staff member, the Reverend David Bailey.

Notice that this is almost 6 percent of the membership of 9,000. It is high, and thereby a sign that Garden Grove Community Church is in good health. Each lay minister of pastoral care is assigned 8-10 families.

This pattern can stretch almost indefinitely. It is the one also used by Pastor Cho Yonggi in Seoul, Korea, which has allowed his church to grow to over 50,000 members in less than 20 years. His 72 associate pastors and 2,600 deacons handle the pastoral work in over 2,000 home-style groups of 8-15 families each.

Gift 4: The Gift of Exhortation

The gift of exhortation, like the gift of pastor, is a person-centered gift. A Christian can manifest it in two ways: in a preaching or teaching situation or in a group encounter; or in a private one-on-one situation which meets the particular need of a particular person at a particular time.

However, the gift of exhortation is different from the gift of pastor in that a flock or a group of people is not involved on the basis of a long-term commitment. A person with the gift of exhortation becomes concerned with the spiritual welfare of a brother or sister for the period of time it takes to help that person, then he or she moves on to another. The gift of exhortation can work with relative strangers, but the pastoral gift cannot. Exhortation and pastoral gifts may, of course, both be part of the same person's gift-mix, and perhaps this is a frequent occurrence. I have no statistical feeling for that matter.

The gift of exhortation is the special ability that God gives to certain members of the Body of Christ to minister words of comfort, consolation, encouragement and counsel to other members of the Body in such a way that they feel helped and healed.

The most prominent biblical example of the gift of exhortation was Paul's associate, Barnabas, who was called "son of consolation" in Acts 4:36. It was Barnabas who took Paul under his wing when the other apostles were skeptical about the validity of his conversion. It was Barnabas who saw the potential in John Mark and picked him up when Paul had rejected him. As Leslie Flynn points out, "Do we realize that had not Barnabas used his gift of encouragement we might be missing half of the New Testament books?"[6] Barnabas never wrote Scripture, but the people he helped did. Paul contributed 13 Epistles, and Mark one Gospel.

All Christians, of course, have a role of caring for one another. Hebrews 3:13 says, "Exhort one another daily." The life-style of Christians in contact with one another should be to counsel and share and encourage at all times. But over and above this, some Christians have a special gift of counseling that should become recognized to the extent that people in the church who are hurting know where to go to find help. When this happens, the Body is in good health. It is a positive growth characteristic.

The pastor himself does not necessarily need the gift of exhortation in order to lead a church into vigorous growth. It, like the gift of pastor, could even be a hindrance to growth if the pastor has it. For example, the United Methodist report on membership trends suggests that one of its growth problems might be the "large number of pastors now serving in the United Methodist Church who have been strongly influenced by an emphasis on their role as a passive counselor. Ministers who operate from this stance are not inclined to confront persons with the claims of the gospel or to press for a decision to unite with the church."[7]

Because of the emphasis made on passive counseling and relational theology during the sixties, some pastors who do not have *gifts* of pastor or exhortation may be overstressing their need to exercise a *role* in these areas. When the implications of suggestions such as those made in the Methodist report are studied, churches may recognize that they must retool and readjust their ministerial priorities at this point, if they are to grow over the next decade.

If this happens, the gift of exhortation is another of those gifts that laymen and laywomen in the church probably have. The gift should be identified and put to use, and the pastor is the one responsible to see that this is done. Sometimes it might be advisable to hire a professional counselor for the church staff if the church is big enough to afford it. But this is not always necessary. The resources for meeting the need for counselors may already be right there in the congregation in the form of the gift of exhortation, waiting to be uncovered and used.

Gift 18: The Gift of Administration

Two other gifts frequently but mistakenly considered necessary for the pastor of a growing church, are the gifts of evangelist and administration. I will postpone discussing the gift of evangelist for the next chapter, but here I would like to touch on the gift of administration.

I like to use "the gift of administration" instead of "the gift of governments," as the King James Version has it in the list of gifts in 1 Corinthians 12 (v. 28), because the word better describes my own interpretation of the gift and its place in a healthy church. A different Greek word used in the list in Romans 12, which is translated as "ruling" in the King James (Rom. 12:8), I am calling the "gift of leadership." In other words, I am distinguishing between the gift of administration and the gift of leadership. I feel that a church-growth pastor can get along without the gift of administration but not without the gift of leadership.

The gift of administration is the special ability that God gives to some members of the Body of Christ which enables them to understand clearly the immediate and long-range goals of a particular unit of the Body of Christ to devise and execute effective plans for the accomplishment of those goals.

The Greek word for administration is the word for helmsman. The helmsman is the person in charge of getting the ship to its destination. That is a perfect description of the person to whom God has given the gift of administration. The helmsman stands between the owner of the ship and the crew. The owner of the ship makes the basic decisions as to what is the purpose of the voyage, where the ship is going, and what it is going to do after it gets there. He also sees that a helmsman is hired and he monitors the competency of the helmsman. The crew, on the other hand, takes orders from the helmsman and does the physical work necessary for the helmsman to get the ship to its destination. When trouble occurs in mid-voyage, the owner is not consulted unless it is a dire emergency. The helmsman is expected to make the decisions necessary to solve problems as they arise so that the goals are accomplished and the ship gets to where the owner wants it.

In this analogy, it is clear to me that the pastor of a

growing church is equivalent to the owner of the ship. He needs to know where the ship should go and why. He needs to locate a helmsman and recruit a crew. But he does not necessarily have to be or even want to be a helmsman, to say nothing about a member of the crew, in order for the total purpose to be accomplished.

Pastors who have a gift of administration can make a church organization hum. They enjoy long hours in the office, overseeing the business matters of the church, relating to staff, making phone calls, closing deals, dictating letters and taking satisfaction in their organization. But pastors who do not enjoy any of the above need not despair. In small churches God may have given gifts of administration to men and women who would love to exercise them as a contribution to the church. Sometimes God provides a church secretary who has the gift. In larger churches a skilled assistant is often added to the staff. For example, my senior pastor, Raymond Ortlund, is one of the majority of pastors who do not have the gift of administration. Recognizing this, he has brought Pastor Kent Tucker, who does have the gift, on the staff as assistant to the pastor. Kent Tucker even drew up a PERT chart for his own wedding! The staff has a business manager as well. There is no problem here with a senior minister who does not have the gift of administration.

Pastor Robert Schuller has seen that each one of his major departments, such as the Institute for Successful Church Leadership, the Hour of Power television program, the Tower of Hope ministries, the New Hope Counseling Center, the Women's Ministries and others, has its own competent administrator in charge. But the total system is now getting so large that he has hired Fred Southard, a successful businessman who has the gift of administration, as a helmsman to take over the management of the whole complex organization.

Pastors Ortlund and Schuller are like owners of the ship. But neither would be successful senior ministers if they themselves became helmsmen and shouldered the administrative responsibilities for their church organizations. Both of them, and thousands of other successful pastors, are thanking God for the total Body of Christ and for His provision of members of the Body who have the gift of administration.

Gift 10: The Gift of Faith

If there are 25 spiritual gifts that a successful pastor of a large, growing church does not need, the remaining two that he does need must be very significant. I believe they are. They are the gift of faith and the gift of leadership.

The gift of faith is the special ability that God gives to some members of the Body of Christ to discern with extraordinary confidence the will and purposes of God for the future of His work.

People with the gift of faith are usually more interested in the future than in history. They are goal-centered possibility thinkers, undaunted by circumstances or suffering or obstacles. They can trust God to remove mountains as 1 Corinthians 13:2 indicates. They, like Noah, can build an ark on dry ground in the face of ridicule and criticism, with no doubt at all that God is going to send a flood.

People with the gift of faith are often highly irritated by criticism, much more, for example, than those with the gift of teaching. They can't bring themselves to understand why anyone would criticize them since they have such complete assurance that what they are doing is God's will. They interpret criticism of them as criticism of God, and therefore they often become impatient with Christian friends who do not go along with them. They typically have difficulty understanding the "system" and why it works as it does to slow down progress. Usually people with the gift of faith have a large amount of courage because they feel deeply that they are in partnership with God, and "if God be for us, who can be against us?" (Rom. 8:31).

The superchurch pastors I know all have this gift. Some call them visionaries or dreamers or promoters. They see where God wants them to go, even though they have no idea at the moment how they are going to get there. Years ago, I was aghast when I first heard Robert Schuller tell of his vision for a "crystal cathedral" in Garden Grove, California. A building of 10,000 pieces of glass, shaped like a diamond, larger than the Notre Dame Cathedral of Paris, with fountains of water down the center aisle—blew my mind. But before I heard about his vision, I had already come to the conclusion that God had given him the gift of faith. If I hadn't been convinced of his gift I would have thought he was nuts. But I took him seriously right from the beginning and my wife and I were among the first to buy one of the pieces of glass when they were offered to the public a couple of years ago. I may not have the gift of faith, but I love to be around and support those who do. I refuse to join the company of Schuller-phobes because I believe that his vision has come from God through the gift of faith.

Schuller reminds me of the late George Muller of Bristol, England, whom I mentioned previously. They are so similar because they are both examples of the gift of faith being demonstrated in their ministries. Muller, a century ago, clearly saw God's will for orphanages and was undaunted by multiplied obstacles, including a 5 million dollar price tag. The money all came in during his lifetime. Schuller today clearly sees God's will for a beautiful sanctuary and likewise is undaunted by a 15 million dollar price tag.

Schuller and Muller are similar in some ways but quite different in others. Muller adopted a policy of never making direct appeals for funds, but his ministry became known and funds poured in. He was fortunate enough to have the gift of intercession to accompany his gift of faith. Schuller takes the opposite approach. He tells of how he engaged a rich man in conversation, challenged him with the vision of the crystal cathedral, looked him in the eye and said, "I need your help. I would like you to give me a million dollars toward the cathedral." The man looked him back and said, "Schuller, if you're crazy enough to ask me for a million dollars, I'm crazy enough to give it to you!" Within a few weeks the million dollar gift was in the bank. George Muller would likely have turned over in his grave. But God, I believe, is pleased with them both.

Projecting the Gift of Faith

People with the gift of faith have a particular temptation that both they and others around them need to be aware of. They may easily fall into the syndrome of gift projection. Kenneth Kinghorn of Asbury Seminary warns that "the person who has the gift of faith should not chide others for their lack of faith. After all, not every Christian possesses this gift."[8]

I have already mentioned how rotten I would feel after reading a biography of George Muller until I understood something about gifts. Sometimes when I listen to Bob Schuller I get a similar message. It sounds like: "If you do what I do, you will accomplish what I accomplish. It's easy." Now through many years of association I have learned a great deal about possibility thinking from Bob Schuller, and it has proven to be valuable in many aspects of my life. But no way would I spend time attempting to dream the kind of dreams that seem so natural and easy for him. David refused to wear Saul's armor, and so do I. I do not regard myself as an "impossibility thinker." I try to be a possibility thinker within the limits of my daily Christian role of faith without feeling one ounce of remorse that God will do the kind of things through me that He is doing through my good friend. The whole body can't be an eye.

Whenever we discuss the gift of faith we tend to bring up names of the notables such as Schuller and Muller. If more space were available we could write a modern-day Hebrews 11 mentioning Ralph Winter and Bill Bright and Oral Roberts and Cameron Townsend and Cho Yonggi who have given public demonstration of their gift of faith often measured by multi-million dollar projects. This could and does easily become discouraging to members of the Body of Christ who have a lesser degree of the gift of faith. But there are many more one- and two-talent people than the five- or ten-talent kind of person.

The average person with the gift of faith in a leadership role in the church may never build a crystal cathedral, but he can discern with a great deal of confidence where God wants that church to be five years or ten years from now. He can set goals. He can establish a mood for growth. Because the pastor believes so strongly in growth, the people find his attitude contagious. They get excited about it. The two basic axioms of church growth are: (1) the pastor must want the church to grow and be willing to pay the price, and (2) the people must want the church to grow and be willing to pay the price. In a church where the pastor has the gift of faith, these two axioms are usually in dynamic operation. The church is ready to grow.

Gift 6: The Gift of Leadership

The gift of faith lets the church-growth pastor know where he should go. The gift of leadership lets him know how to get there.

The gift of leadership is the special ability that God gives to certain members of the Body of Christ to set goals in accordance with God's purpose for the future and to communicate these goals to others in such a way that they voluntarily and harmoniously work together to accomplish those goals for the glory of God.

Leaders must have followers. If leadership quality is due to a gift (in contrast to some legal power) their followers will be voluntary. Whereas discerning leaders never get too far ahead of their followers, they are always up front directing others. Gifted leaders neither manipulate nor coerce. They generate a confidence that they know where they are going and what the next step is to get there. Most people want to be led.

The best leaders are relaxed. They know what has to be done and they know they cannot do it themselves. So they develop skills in delegating and transferring responsibilities to others. Many leaders dislike administration, so they make sure they have delegated that responsibility to someone who has a different gift-mix. Lyle Schaller likens skillful pastors of growing churches to "ranchers" rather than "shepherds." Ranchers make sure that their different flocks and herds get the attention they need, and they get others to do it. They take little personal interest in the problems of the individual sheep. Pastors who prefer the shepherd model will have to content themselves with small churches, and this may well be God's will for them. In them, their role of leadership will suffice without a special gift. On the other hand those who can fit into the rancher model have much greater possibilities for growth. They are likely to have the gift of leadership. God loves both shepherds and ranchers.

Longevity and Philosophy of Ministry

It takes time to establish leadership in a church, even when the pastor has the gift. This is the main reason why pastoral longevity has been found to be directly related to church growth. A common thread running through the testimonies of pastors of churches that have established a reputation for excellence and growth is that they have received a lifetime call to that church. Neither they nor their people are wondering where they will be five years from now. Their commitment to each other is reminiscent of a marriage agreement—until death do us part. Lyle Schaller puts it this way: "One of the means of reducing the positive impact of pastoral leadership is to change ministers every few years."[9] He goes on to say that the most productive years of a pastor usually begin only after the fourth to sixth year of the minister's tenure.

Changing pastors frequently prevents a church from establishing a firm philosophy of ministry, now recognized as an important factor for health and growth. Each church needs to be able to articulate why it is there and why it is not the same as other churches in the same area or in the same denomination. Few churches, however, have been able to establish their philosophy of ministry because pastoral leadership is usually needed to do it well. When pastors come and go frequently, philosophies of ministry usually come and go as well.

When there is a long-term pastoral commitment, the philosophy of ministry can and should be built around the spiritual gifts of the senior minister. Growing churches are doing this. In the Los Angeles area, for example, Pastors John MacArthur and Charles Swindoll have the gift of teaching. Their churches, Grace Community (Panorama City) and Evangelical Free (Fullerton), have a philosophy of ministry called "classroom churches." Pastor Ralph Wilkerson on the other hand, has the gift of evangelist and so his Melodyland Christian Center is built as an evangelistic center, vastly different from a classroom church.

Pastoral leadership for growth depends on the pastor and people agreeing where they are going and being committed to each other to get there. Growth potential is limited unless the person called to head up the church has the gift of leadership. By no means can just anybody who has a seminary degree pull it off.

The Pastor's Roles

By accepting the position as the pastor of a Christian church, a person has committed himself or herself to a life of demanding work. Not only must a pastor discover and develop and use his own spiritual gifts but, even in the best of situations, he must be prepared to exercise his Christian roles to a degree much higher than the average Christian. This cannot be avoided.

If the pastor does not develop a "spiritual gifts dynamic" among the members of the congregation, the demands on his roles can easily become excessive. Ray Stedman laments that pastors have been assigned the task of "evangelizing the world, counseling the distressed and brokenhearted, ministering to the poor and needy, relieving the oppressed and afflicted, expounding the Scriptures, and challenging the entrenched forces of evil in an increasingly darkened world." He points out that pastors were never meant to do all this, and "to even attempt it is to end up frustrated, exhausted, and emotionally drained."[10] Is he describing your pastor?

Few things make the pastoral task more enjoyable than a congregation in which spiritual gifts are in operation. The pastor becomes the coach of the team. He is doing what he likes to do and doing it well. Growth possibilities are almost unlimited. The body is functioning as it was designed to function by its maker.

Ministerial Training and Spiritual Gifts

Once it is recognized that the pastor is the key person for church growth, the training of that pastor becomes a crucial consideration. The United Presbyterian study of membership trends, for example, found that as far as the pastor is concerned, his caliber of leadership is the most important determinative to church growth. While recognizing the dangers of "clericalism," the report goes on to say that "upgrading the quality of the professional leadership is essential to developing and enabling a congregation to grow."[11] This brings up the question of how the training is accomplished.

Most ministers in the United States are trained in Bible school or seminary. The Bible school is post-secondary level and the seminary is post-college level. Both are set up on a pre-service model and neither bases its programs on spiritual gifts.

What do I mean by this? Christians, as we have seen, are supposed to discover, develop and use their spiritual gifts. The purpose of the professional training that is offered in Bible schools and seminaries is to prepare Christian ministers. But one of the basic problems is that, generally speaking, the people who enter those institutions have not yet discovered their spiritual gifts and had them confirmed in any significant way by the

Body of Christ. Since they have never been in the ministry, there is no way for them to know for sure whether they have a gift-mix appropriate for pastoral work. Seminary application forms do not screen out candidates who are unsure that they have the kind of ministry gifts that seminaries are set up to help develop. The all too prevalent assumption is that by virtue of taking a three- or four-year course in Bible school or seminary, people can be trained to be pastors no matter what gift-mix God has given them.

To complicate matters, the faculties of these institutions are typically staffed mostly by scholars rather than by practicing ministers, even though professional training is designed to produce ministers. Because like tends to beget like, the models that the students observe while they are studying is that of Christian scholars. Very frequently, new seminary graduates are surprised to discover that the members of their churches are not very interested in the scholarly theological and exegetical problems about which they wrote their term papers. They then find themselves poorly equipped to resolve interpersonal conflicts, heal people who are hurting, put broken marriages back together, diagnose the health of their church, or set growth goals for the next five years.

A third growth-restricting feature of the typical seminary program is that it extracts the student from the real world for an extended period of time, socializes him or her in an academic context removed from the parish except for marginal "practical work" assignments, credentials him as a professional minister, and sends him into a world he has only experienced incidentally or vicariously. The resulting culture shock is often overwhelming, and some never recover from it.

I have a dream to correct this that I share whenever possible.[12]

I should think that seminaries, if they decided to restructure on the basis of developing spiritual gifts, would extend the current three-year Master of Divinity program to something more like 15 years. The only students then would be part-time. They would be making their living in the ministry in some parish situation where they would definitely be testing their ministry gift-mix. They would study their subjects much as older ministers now study in Doctor of Ministry programs at seminaries: mostly independent study with periodic seminars lasting two weeks or so, either on the campus of the institution or in extension centers nearer to clusters of students.

Present curricula would not have to change much, except to allow more credit for studying at the in-church seminars now offered by many successful church leaders across the country. I could see tremendous benefit for any seminary student preparing for the parish ministry to take seminars with Jack Hyles of First Baptist, Hammond, Indiana, or with Ray Stedman of Peninsula Bible Church, Palo Alto, California, or with G.L. Johnson of Peoples Church, Fresno, California or with W.A. Criswell of First Baptist, Dallas, Texas, or with Jack Hayford of Church on the Way, Van Nuys, California, or with Robert Schuller of Garden Grove, California, or with Bill Yaeger of First Baptist, Modesto, California, or with any number of other successful ministers who have developed ways and means of sharing their knowledge and experience in extra-seminary situations. Some seminaries are beginning to offer credit for these field training experiences, and their numbers, hopefully, will multiply.

I am not naive enough to think that these suggestions are going to be welcomed with open arms by the educational establishment. Present procedures are too deeply entrenched. But, who knows? Better days may be ahead.

Interns and Homegrown Staff

Two growing trends in American churches give me some hope that better things are ahead for training ministers. One is a growing awareness of the value of internship programs. Some churches are particularly skilled at taking seminary students on their staff and supplementing their seminary training with practical involvement under the supervision of senior ministers and staff members who are gifted to do this. Internship programs need to be multiplied and intensified, particularly in growing churches. Internship programs in plateaued or declining churches can be counterproductive. In such situations, poor church health can be considered normal, especially if the senior minister has developed competence in rationalizing non-growth in biblical and theological terms.

A second trend is that of recruiting new church staff members from the existing congregation rather than seeking help from the outside. This kind of recruitment is done strictly on the basis of spiritual gifts that have already been discovered by the individual and confirmed by the Body. The new staff members are mature. They know and live the philosophy of ministry of the church. They have accepted the senior minister as their leader and count themselves as loyal followers and supporters. The fact that they do not have a seminary degree seems to be of lesser importance. In many cases they enroll in nearby seminaries or Bible schools and get their theological training on the kind of long-term, continuing education basis as we previously suggested.

Such well-known churches as Grace Community Church of the Valley, Panorama City, California; Grace Chapel, Lexington, Massachusetts; Lake Avenue Congregational, Pasadena, California; Garden Grove Community Church, Garden Grove, California and many others are doing this. First Baptist of Modesto, California, for example, has recruited 15 of 17 staff members from their own congregation. Their staff members include a former carpet store owner, peach farmer, furniture salesman, Sears manager, tire store manager, savings and loan manager, building contractor and mayor of Modesto, no less. I have heard about so many churches starting to recruit homegrown staff members within the last three years that I now see it as a national trend. If it is, I believe it will have a tremendously beneficial effect on church growth, and it may also force the educational institutions to design more of their programs to meet the need for training mature people who have switched careers later on in life. This, in turn, will tend to upgrade the quality of ministerial leadership in the country as a whole because it will be more in tune with the Body of Christ and its spiritual gifts.

Notes

1. Warren H. Hartman, *Membership Trends: A Study of Decline and Growth in the United Methodist Church 1949-1975*, (Nashville: Discipleship Resources, 1976), p. 44.
2. United Presbyterian Church, *A Summary Report of the Committee on Membership Trends* (New York, 1976), p. 19.
3. Dan Martin, "The Church Growth Questions," *Home Missions* (December, 1977), p. 12.
4. David A. Roozen, *Church Membership and Participation: Trends, Determinants and Implications for Policy and Planning* (Hartford: Hartford Seminary Foundation, 1978), p. 58.
5. For a more thorough discussion of the celebration-congregation- cell concept see C. Peter Wagner, *Your Church Can Grow* (Glendale: Regal Books, 1976), pp. 97-109; and from a slightly different perspective, Lyle E. Shaller, *Assimilating New Members* (Nashville: Abingdon Press, 1978), pp. 69-96.
6. Leslie B. Flynn, *Nineteen Gifts of the Spirit* (Wheaton: Victor Books, 1974), p. 88.
7. Hartman, *Membership Trends*, p. 44.
8. Kenneth Cain Kinghorn, *Gifts of the Spirit* (Nashville: Abingdon Press, 1976), p. 67.
9. Schaller, *Assimilating New Members*, p. 53.
10. Ray C. Stedman, *Body Life* (Glendale: Regal Books, 1972), p. 79.
11. United Presbyterian Church, *A Summary Report*, p. 19.
12. For an elaboration of this concept, see C. Peter Wagner, "Seminaries Ought to Be Asking Who as Well as How," *Theological Education* (Summer, 1974), pp. 266-279.

6.
The Evangelist: The Primary Organ for Growth

Every separate bodily function has primary and secondary organs which, working together, accomplish the task. If this is true of the human body, I do not believe we stretch the apostle Paul's analogy of the physical body too far if we postulate that for given church functions the Body of Christ has been provided with primary and secondary organs.

Take reproduction, for example. That is the physical function nearest to evangelism in the church. Reproduction adds new members to the human race while evangelism adds new members to the Body of Christ.

Obviously the primary organ for accomplishing the task of human reproduction is the uterus. But when you think of it, the most perfect uterus God ever created could not reproduce if it were not for the simultaneous activity of the digestive system, the respiratory system, the endocrine system, the nervous system, and the circulatory system. While the uterus is the primary organ for reproduction, it is worthless without the healthy activity of the secondary organs.

The application to spiritual gifts is self-evident. The gift of evangelist is the primary organ that God has provided for reproduction. But the finest gift of evangelist in Christendom will not help churches to grow if the other members of the Body, the secondary organs for church growth, are not also functioning in a healthy manner.

This brings us back to the observation we have made on numerous other occasions: church growth and church health are interrelated. Only healthy bodies grow well, and only healthy churches grow well. Conversely, healthy churches can be expected to grow—it is one of the signs of good health. Statements such as, "Our church is losing members, but we are healthy," do not square with all the biblical data as to what God expects from the Body of Christ. One of the healthy church models we have in the New Testament is the Jerusalem church following Pentecost. Among other signs of good health, the Lord was adding daily such as should be saved (see Acts 2:47). If the Lord is not regularly adding new members, something is wrong with the church.

All church growth is not equally good growth. Although there are exceptions, the most beneficial kind of growth is conversion growth. That is what Acts 2:47 refers to. This is also called Kingdom growth because new members are being brought into the Kingdom of God. The gift of evangelist is only marginally necessary for biological growth, not necessary at all for transfer growth, but exceedingly important for conversion growth.

Gift 19: The Gift of Evangelist

The gift of evangelist is mentioned in the list in Ephesians 4:11. In that context, as pointed out previously, it specifically refers to the office of evangelist. But since in the same list the prophet is presumed to have the gift of prophecy and the apostle the gift of apostle and the teacher the gift of teaching, it does not seem to be far-fetched to suppose that the evangelist is presumed to have the spiritual gift of evangelist.

The gift of evangelist is the special ability that God gives to certain members of the Body of Christ to share the gospel with unbelievers in such a way that men and women become Jesus' disciples and responsible members of the Body of Christ.

The process of discovering this gift is the same as that for any other. Experiment, examine your feelings, evaluate your effectiveness, and expect confirmation from the Body.

One of today's great evangelists, Leighton Ford, tells how he discovered his gift in his excellent book, *Good News Is for Sharing*. "As a boy of sixteen," he says, "I first met Billy Graham and other gifted evangelists through the Youth for Christ movement. Observing these men and women in action, both personally and publicly, I felt something stirring within me. A longing to express my faith grew. Opportunities came to speak at youth groups and then at small evangelistic occasions. People were moved to accept Christ through what I said. While I believe God has given me certain other spiritual gifts, the gift of evangelism is primary."[1]

How Leighton Ford feels about his total spiritual life in light of what he recognizes as his primary gift is later expressed in these words: "I have discovered that it is only as I fan my gift into flame that I find fulfillment and growth in other areas of my Christian life."[2]

I like the advice that Rick Yohn, pastor of the Evangelical Free Church of Fresno, California gives to people in his church who are anxious to learn whether they have the gift of evangelist. He asks them two questions: (1) Do you have a strong desire to share your faith with others? I'm not asking whether you want to see people come to Christ. Most Christians want to see a life changed. But do you personally enjoy talking to others about Christ? The second question, (2) Are you seeing results?[3]

So far we have mentioned Leighton Ford and Billy Graham as well-known figures with the gift of evangelist. But they certainly are not to be considered as the only, or even the main, kind of person who has been given the gift. They are so well-known because they are full-time public professional evangelists, some of the very few in relationship to the total Body of Christ. Here are some of the other varieties the gift of evangelist can assume:

1. Man or woman.
2. Layperson or professional.
3. Ordained or unordained.
4. Full-time or part-time.
5. Personal or public.
6. Denominational or interdenominational.
7. Monocultural or cross-cultural.
8. Existing churches or starting new churches.

The above list is certainly not exhaustive. One could think of Charles E. Fuller who was not only a public evangelist, but one who made particularly effective use of the medium of radio. Others are skilled in evangelizing through literature or music or even basketball. God has provided a large variety of ways that the gift of evangelist can be manifested.

What Does Evangelism Really Mean?

No matter how it is exercised, the objective of the gift of evangelist is the same: to bring people to a commitment to Jesus Christ and a commitment to each other in the Body of Christ.

This statement presupposes a certain definition of evangelism that is not yet fully accepted even by evangelicals. It is a position that is not satisfied with the *presence* definition so prevalent in the more liberal branches of Christianity. To *presence* people, evangelism is accomplished when a cup of cold water is given in the name of Jesus whether or not the gospel is made clear to the recipient.

Neither is the definition satisfied with adding *proclamation* to presence, although many evangelicals hold tenaciously to that position. They argue that biblical evangelism is accomplished when the good news is faithfully *proclaimed* and understood, whether or not people become disciples of Jesus Christ.

The above definition of evangelism does not include *discipleship*. To report your results under such a definition, you report how many people heard the message and how many made decisions for Christ of one kind or another. A third definition, which I believe is the most helpful one for church growth, warmly accepts the essential need for both presence and proclamation, but holds that the evangelistic process remains incomplete unless and until the person being evangelized has not only made a decision, but has also proved that he or she is a disciple of Jesus by a visible commitment to the Body of Christ in some form or other. Some refer to this definition as the *persuasion* view.[4] It regards people who have heard the gospel and rejected it as still unevangelized and as important targets for future evangelistic efforts.

Proclaiming the gospel does not particularly require a spiritual gift. But, since salvation is so completely a work of the Holy Spirit, proclaiming the gospel with unusual effectiveness so that regularly, week in and week out, new people come to faith in Christ and commitment to the Body, does require supernatural help through a spiritual gift.

How Many Have the Gift of Evangelist?

It goes without saying that not all members of the Body of Christ have the gift of evangelist. The whole body is not intended to be an eye (see 1 Cor. 12:17), much less a uterus. In fact, as we suggested in chapter 2, a minority of the bodily members have been given any one gift. This in itself narrows down the answer to the question as to how many have the gift to something between 1 and 49 percent.

Of course, all the gifts are not evenly distributed. We have two eyes, 10 toes, one stomach, and 32 teeth. That is why it would be silly to figure that because there are 27 different gifts an average of 3.7 percent of the members of the Body would have any one gift. The spiritual organism is much more complex than that. But I find that the general tendency of Christians enthusiastic about getting certain tasks done in the Body is to carelessly overestimate how many of the members should have one gift or another. If I want my particular job to get done well I might tend to presume that an unrealistic number of people have the gift it takes. This happens frequently with the gift of evangelist.

So far in this book I have suggested only one figure for estimating the number of people who have a certain gift. I said that those with the gift of pastor will probably number between 3 and 6 percent depending on some variables which were explained in chapter 5. I stated that only as a rule of thumb because I feel that more research needs to be done on the pastoral gift, as well as on the others.

I am much more secure in my present suggestion on the percentage for the gift of evangelist because over a period of years it has been tested in case after case and found to stand up. The average Christian church can realistically expect that approximately 10 percent of its active adult members will have been given the gift of evangelist. A mounting quantity of empirical evidence indicates that if a church has 10 percent, or even a few percentage points less than 10 percent, of its active members mobilized for evangelism, a growth pattern of 200 percent per decade is a realistic expectation. If God blesses a church by giving the gift of evangelism to more than 10 percent of its members, it is in wonderful shape for growth.

Can Evangelism Be Overemphasized?

Evangelism is so important for church growth that one can understand why many Christian circles tend to overemphasize it. Overemphasize?

Before I answer this, I need to stress that I personally believe in evangelism so much that I have dedicated my life to see that it happens on a world scale. My personalized California license plate is MT 28:19 and my wife's MT 28:20—the Great Commission wherever we go. I have already stressed that the gift of evangelist is the primary organ in the Body of Christ for church growth. My objective in this book, as in every book I write, is to facilitate the evangelization of the world in our generation. I do not want to be misinterpreted on this matter in the slightest, because what I am about to say may be controversial.

In order to evangelize the world more effectively in our generation, I believe that many evangelicals need to get their heads out of the clouds when it comes to pronouncements about the degree of involvement that the average Christian ought to have in active evangelistic work. There are certain basic things that we need to recognize. For one thing every true Christian has got to be in tune with God who is "not willing that any should perish, but that all should come to repentance" (2 Pet. 3:9). Every Christian desires to see people saved and brought into the fellowship of the Body. This is not the issue.

For another thing, every true Christian is a witness for Jesus Christ whether he or she has the gift of evangelist or not. Furthermore every Christian needs to be prepared to share his or her faith with unbelievers and lead them to Christ whenever the opportunity presents itself. This is the Christian role that corresponds to this spiritual gift, and I will discuss it in more detail shortly.

But having said this, it is time we admitted that there are many good, faithful, consecrated, mature Christian people who are in love with Jesus Christ but who are not, do not care to be, and for all intents and purposes will not be significantly involved in evangelization in any direct way. Indirectly, yes. They will contribute to the growth of the Body of Christ like the lungs and the small intestines and the kidneys and the thyroid gland contribute to human reproduction. And they will carry out their role of witness when circumstances so dictate. But they won't go around looking for opportunities to share their faith.

It is a misunderstanding of biblical teaching, in my opinion, to try to convince every Christian that he or she has to be sharing the faith constantly as a part of their duty to the Master. We do not tell them that they have to teach all the time or pastor others all the time or be an apostle or a prophet or an administrator or a leader or a missionary if they haven't been given the spiritual equipment to do the job well. To make people feel guilty if they ever get gas and don't share Christ with the filling station attendant or if they don't leave tracts for the mailman or if they don't witness to the waitress in the restaurant may actually harm the Body of Christ more than help it.

A recent study was done of Conservative Baptist seminary students who we can presume are representative of average or slightly above average Christians in their spiritual life and commitment, if perhaps somewhat lower in maturity. Certainly their honesty is commendable, given the excessive pressures that have been put on Christians to share their faith at all times. Of the sample studied it was discovered that 10 percent of them share their faith once a week or more, and 10 percent of them have led one to three people to Christ within the past year. The others in varying degrees indicated that (a) they have few contacts with non-Christians, (b) they do not desire help so they can relate better to non-Christians, (c) they probably wouldn't bring unsaved friends to most church functions, (d) they don't want to learn to evangelize, (e) they feel they should lead people to Christ, but they don't want to give much time and energy to it, and (f) their prayer concern is high, but they don't spend much time actually praying for the unsaved.

Independently of this, but part of the same phenomenon, is a report from the Conservative Baptist Home Mission Board passed in June, 1973, expressing concern that the missionary candidates coming from the seminaries score high on the gifts of pastor and teacher, but low on the gift of evangelism.

How do we react to such a situation?

Some tend to tear their hair out, dress in sackcloth and ashes, and lament the low spiritual condition of our young people today. I tend to regard that situation as something that can and should be improved, but not something that is necessarily devastating to church health and church growth.

A key to relating the dynamic of the spiritual gift of evangelist to church growth lies in the question of the location of guilt. Guilt can be a blessing or it can be a curse, depending on where it is located.

First, Christians who have the gift of evangelist and who are not using their gift should be made to feel a responsibility for using it. If 10 percent have the gift, in probably the majority of churches that are plateaued or declining, only about 0.5 percent of the people are using the gift, if that many. That means that 9.5 percent of the people should probably feel guilty if they are not evangelizing and evangelizing strenuously. Those with the gift of exhortation should seek these people out and help them discover, develop and use their gift. They will be happier and more fulfilled Christians and the church will grow. If this produces guilt it will undoubtedly be a blessing.

Second, the 90 percent who have gifts other than that of evangelist should not be allowed to feel guilty if they assume secondary roles in the evangelistic process. This is where God intended them to be, or He would have given them the gift of evangelist. In some evangelical churches the guilt trip for not evangelizing is so severe that when the 10 percent do evangelize and bring new people into the church the converts are turned off by what they find. The general tone of the body, the negative self-image of the members, the gloom and defeatism that can be felt in the atmosphere of the church makes them think that everybody must have been baptized in vinegar! They quickly decide that they want no part of a crowd like that and soon vanish, unnoticed, out the back door.

Projecting the Gift of Evangelist

In light of what has been said, it is easily understood why the gift of evangelist is probably the most frequently projected of all the gifts (with the possible exception of the gift of tongues).

In my experience, the most common technique used by those who have the gift of evangelist for projecting their gift is to deny that they have the gift. Most American Christians who are aware of their ministry agree that two of the most outstanding Christian leaders with the gift of evangelist today are Bill Bright, president of Campus Crusade for Christ, and James Kennedy, senior minister of Coral Ridge Presbyterian Church, Fort Lauderdale, Florida, and founder of Evangelism Explosion. They are both personal friends of mine. I have observed them as carefully as I can. My considered opinion is that they both have the gift, they have developed it to a high degree, and they are using it for the glory of God and the growth of the church. I love them both. I love to spend time with them. I love to hear them tell of their experiences in sharing Christ and inspiring others to do the same. I publicly endorse the programs they have developed as excellent methodologies for local church evangelism.

The reason I mention these two leaders, however, is that I have heard each of them say that he does not have the gift of evangelist. For a long time I was haunted with the question: Why would they deny such a thing?

As I write this, I know that they both will disagree with what I am saying. I hope they don't get irritated with me. We have discussed spiritual gifts at length one-on-one, and both of them feel that my way of presenting the hypothesis that 10 percent of the members of the Body of Christ have the gift of evangelist will be snatched up and used as a cop-out by Christians all over America. They basically feel that the notion that only those with the gift of evangelist ought to be evangelizing in a planned and structured way is erroneous, and that every Christian worth his or her spiritual salt ought to be using the Four Spiritual Laws regularly or be active in an Evangelism Explosion program, or the equivalent of either.

Virtually every time I am with Bill Bright for more than 10 minutes at a time he tells me moving stories of how God used him to lead people to Christ. Once he told me about a waitress in a restaurant in an Asian country who met Christ while he and his wife, Vonnette, were eating there. He told me about a hotel maid who prayed to receive Christ. He has told me about several people on airplane seats next to him whom he has introduced to Jesus.

And here I am, an ordinary seminary professor with the gift of scholar-teacher, completely at a loss to match him story for story. Who wants to hear about the outline for a new magazine article, or a difficult concept made simple on an overhead slide, or a doctoral student who made a breakthrough in his dissertation, or a new book just released by a faculty colleague or that 50 students enrolled for a new seminar in church growth? If I were back in the days before I had come to terms with my own gift-mix, I might still be choked up with guilt when I hear these soul-winning stories.

But no longer. Perhaps Bright and Kennedy will say,

"I told you so, Wagner's copping out!" But here's what I do on an airplane.

As I said previously, I believe that a Christian who knows his or her gift-mix ought to structure as much time as possible to use that gift or gifts. Whenever I get on an airplane, I consider myself in a library. For three or four or five uninterrupted hours I have a beautiful chance to use my spiritual gifts. No telephone calls, no mail delivery, no knocks on the door. I take 8 to 12 pounds of reading material in my brief case because if I am going to use my gift of knowledge (scholar) I have to put in the time reading quantities of books and journals and magazines which I do voraciously. I look for a seat where no one is in the same row and consider it a good flight if I am all alone. If someone sits next to me, I make it a habit to pray and ask the Lord to keep that person quiet unless he or she has a heart that He has prepared for the gospel message. If so I ask the Lord to open a conversation about Jesus. There are plenty of opportunities because people can tell I'm a Christian immediately when they see what I am studying and see me say grace when the meal is served. In fact when we do converse, the other person has usually already figured out that I'm a minister of some kind.

But more often than not, I don't converse with the person beside me because I am too busy using my spiritual gift. The Lord is not going to hold me responsible for what I did as an evangelist, but He is going to hold me responsible for what I did as a scholar-teacher. On the other hand those with the gift of evangelist should make every effort to converse with the people next to them on the plane.

It is difficult for those who have a gift to understand the feelings of those who do not have it and who are made to feel guilty because they don't have it. I have talked to several Campus Crusade staff members, for example, who are suffering guilt feelings for not having the gift of evangelist but who feel that they are expected to show on their weekly reports that they are witnessing with the same effectiveness as other staff members who have the gift. One who has explained in writing how this worked in his life is Rick Yohn, author of one of our top 10 books on spiritual gifts.

Rick Yohn tells about the frustrations that plagued him while he worked on the Campus Crusade staff. "I would hear about other staff workers introducing students to Christ," he says, "and I would compare their results with mine. They always saw greater numerical results." This bothered Rick Yohn deeply, and he searched his heart before God. "Was I lacking faith?" he would ask. He honestly did not believe so. Some did respond, but not many. Then he asked, "Was my message deficient?" The answer to that one obviously was no because he used the same Four Spiritual Laws that the more successful staff members used.

At that point Yohn had to conclude, "Either I am a complete failure as a minister or my gifts are in an area other than evangelism." He found that his basic gift-mix was pastor-teacher, and he has enjoyed ministering that gift for the glory of God ever since. Even though he has served in three pastorates, he still sees few people coming to Christ through his ministry. But he is liberated. He now thinks it's a shame when spirituality is judged on the basis of how many souls a person has won.[5]

I myself consciously try to avoid gift projection. I would not want to judge the spirituality of other Christians on the basis of whether they had a Ph.D. or whether they had become fluent in the vernacular of a second culture, qualities that my gifts of knowledge and missionary require of me. I try not to get disturbed when

I see some teach and know that they are not communicating with the listeners. I try not to be disdainful if someone I am conversing with does not understand the meaning of "theological contextualization" or "homogeneity" or "radical discipleship" or "assimilationist racism" or "dynamic equivalence" because they have not been reading and studying the books I have. If I did engage in such gift projection, I might suspect that I was not obeying the Golden Rule and doing unto others as I would have them do unto me.

Is This a Cop-Out?

I agree with Leighton Ford, an evangelist who is willing to recognize his own evangelistic gift. While he admits that God makes certain people evangelists through spiritual gifts, he also says, "We must not use the teaching of spiritual gifts as a cop-out to avoid our responsibility to share Christ with others. You may not be called as an evangelist, but you and every Christian, by an attitude of love, by compassionate concern, and by well-chosen words, can have the privilege to lead others . . . toward Jesus Christ."[6] This is very timely advice.

Leighton Ford refers here to what we have been calling the Christian role. Every Christian is called to be a faithful witness of Jesus Christ. David Hubbard, president of Fuller Seminary, tells it this way:

"Not all of us have the gift of evangelism. I admire people who can lead others to Jesus Christ right on the spot, who have the ability to turn every conversation into an occasion for sharing God's plan of salvation. I am not one of those, but I have a story to share—and so do you. I have a relationship with Christ that I can describe—and so do you. Evangelism will best take place when all of God's people have learned to express their winsome witness."[7]

I have found this is to be true in my own life. If, when I am on an airplane, God answers my prayer by opening up a conversation with the person next to me, all the books and notes and magazines go back into the brief case and I give my full attention to witnessing. Out comes the Bible I always carry with me, and I share Christ. I know how to do this (sometimes I use the Four Spiritual Laws, sometimes I use the Evangelism Explosion questions) and I know how to lead people to Christ. I have led a person to Christ right there on the airplane seat next to me, and have marked it down as a red letter day.

My role as a Christian is to be a witness for my Lord at any time, and I am delighted when God gives me the opportunity. But I have found that whenever I force it, I blow it. So I let God do it for me. When He doesn't, I stick to exercising my spiritual gift rather than my Christian role.

Whoever uses his or her lack of having the spiritual gift of evangelist as a cop-out from witnessing displeases God. But whoever insists that another person divert valuable energy that could be used for exercising a spiritual gift into feebly executing a Christian role likewise displeases God.

New Converts and Effective Witness

Contrary to what some would expect, the more mature a Christian becomes in the faith, the less potential that person has as an effective witness. The main reason for this is that an increasing involvement with the Body of Christ over a period of time steadily reduces the number of contacts a person has with unbelievers. Before a person is a Christian all his or her friends and relatives may be non-Christians. The same is true for new converts before they have become well assimilated into the family of God. Possibilities for the use of the role of witness are usually very high but only for a limited period of time after a person becomes a Christian.

If the role of witness is ever to be structured for church growth, here is the area to concentrate on. New Christians, before they mature enough to discover what their spiritual gifts are, should be encouraged by every means to use their remaining contacts with unsaved friends and relatives for evangelistic purposes. But in most cases they will not know how to lead others to Christ very well. Chances are, 9 out of 10 have not been given the gift of evangelist. It seems to me, therefore, that the strongest kind of mobilization for evangelism in a church is to combine these 10 percent of the mature Christians who do have the gift of evangelist with the new converts who have a role of witness and to introduce their friends and relatives to Jesus Christ through that kind of teamwork.

This recently happened in my own congregation, the Voyagers Sunday School Class. One of the members of the class, Steve Lazarian, has the gift of evangelist along with his wife, Iris. He owns an electrical contracting business. A few months ago they met a man also in the electrical business who had been transferred here from back East and they led him to the Lord. He then witnessed the best way he could to his wife and to the people at his office. Soon he brought a woman from his office to class, then she brought a friend of hers, then his wife became interested. He got them all together with the Lazarians and the Lazarians led all three to Christ. In the past six months the Voyagers have grown 6 percent, a good rate of growth for any congregation.

For this dynamic to operate smoothly, of course, there needs to be a steady supply of new converts in the church. Some churches, however, don't like new converts that much and they telegraph their attitude in subtle ways. New converts are something like babies around the house—a nuisance when it comes right down to it. But, like babies, they are nuisances that should be loved and nurtured. They should not be expected to behave like mature Christians, but if they are made to feel welcome and cared for in every way they will quickly mature. Before they do, however, their role of witness and their contacts with unbelievers should be cultivated with diligence. Churches that know how to do that usually grow well.

We need to recognize in passing that second-generation Christians, sons and daughters of active church members who come into the church through what is called biological growth, usually will not be highly effective in their role of witness. Some of them undoubtedly will have the gift of evangelist, and they may discover it fairly early, which is a plus. But otherwise they cannot be depended upon for accomplishing much evangelism, and it is not usually advisable to build an evangelistic program around them.

Building a Dynamic for Outreach

How does a church grow that uses team combinations of those with the gift of evangelist and those with the role of witness who still have effective contacts with unbelievers? There are two target areas to begin work on this: (1) new members and (2) older members of the church. Concurrently there are two objectives: (1) to help those who have the gift of evangelist to discover, develop and begin to use their gift; and (2) to equip the others who have a role of Christian witness to be more effective in their witnessing.

Target area 1: new members. I believe that new members, as a part of the membership class or whatever the process for receiving new members is called in your church, ought to be required to go through formal training in sharing their faith. The training ought to include some on-the-job experience in evangelism. I realize that this is a fairly radical suggestion, and I have not been surprised that, although I have suggested it to numerous pastors over the past five years, none that I know of has actually implemented my suggestion.

Perhaps the main reason why this suggestion has not caught on in a big way is that pastors and staffs and church boards are too timid. They do not understand this very important principle of sociology of religion: the stricter a church is in its membership requirements, the more religious and social strength it will gain in the community. No one has articulated this and developed it more extensively than Dean Kelley in his book, *Why Conservative Churches Are Growing.*[8] I recommend the book highly for its simplicity, realism and common sense. I would like every pastor and church board member in America to read it. It would greatly help to dispel fears that the church will not grow as well if it increases membership requirements.

Dean Kelley's definition of strictness has many facets. One of them is the one I am suggesting—a deep-seated desire to share the faith and win converts. By making this a component intrinsic to the membership process, your church will flash the clear message to the world that it is an evangelistic church, that it cares about those who are yet unsaved, and that being a member of your church means being part of a Body that is determined to add new members and grow on a regular basis. Few things could contribute more to the total strength of the church in the community.

There are many excellent ways to learn to share the

faith now available to the Christian public, and undoubtedly more will be developed. Organizations such as Evangelism Explosion, Campus Crusade for Christ, Churches Alive, the Navigators and others have developed expertise in providing this kind of training. The method should be carefully chosen because some fit better into certain church types than others. Some denominations also have their own kinds of programs for local church evangelism and outreach, and these might be just what the doctor ordered. But whatever the methodology, if such training is made a part of the requirements for church membership, both for those who transfer in and for those who are converted from the world, the whole church will benefit greatly.

After suggesting this for some time, I was delighted when I discovered that at least one church had already been doing it. College Hill Presbyterian Church of Cincinnati, Ohio is a model that needs to be studied closely. The senior minister is Jerry Kirk. With his encouragement and under the direct leadership of the Minister of Evangelism, Ron Rand, the church, which has around 2,000 members, began to require training in evangelism for its new members in 1973. Over the previous four years attendance had been showing a decadal rate of decline of minus 4 percent. But then the four year period from 1973 through 1976 it showed a decadal growth rate of 109 percent! Their program is called HELPER, an acronym for "How to Equip Lay People to Evangelize Regularly." It is not the only requirement for church membership, but it is one important part of it. In the HELPER training program several different methods of sharing the faith are taught to the people.

College Hill Presbyterian Church does not fear that higher standards for membership will hurt church growth. They have found through experience that high membership standards will do just the opposite. The church has become stronger by making it harder to get in. Now others are considering doing the same. College Hill shares what it has learned in three clinics per year held on their Cincinnati campus and in other regional clinics which Ron Rand is willing to set up, upon invitation from a host church.

Target area 2: current members. It is not easy to establish "requirements" for current church members as it is for receiving new members. But I suggest that all current members be encouraged as strongly as possible to experiment with as many spiritual gifts as they can, and that the gift of evangelist be one of the areas where special help is made available. I would put as many current members as possible through an evangelism training program of one kind or another.

College Hill has also done this. Their pastoral leadership has set as a goal putting 100 percent of the membership through the HELPER program. For one thing, it has become an unwritten regulation that church officers in College Hill must have gone through the HELPER program before they are elected to office. At this writing 44 percent of the members have taken the training, a remarkably high figure and a good example for other churches to follow if they decide to take church growth seriously.

Do you see what such a system does to spiritual gifts? It works positively for both those who have the gift of evangelist and those who have other spiritual gifts. Of course, the process must be undertaken in prayer and dependency on the leading of the Holy Spirit. Before people go into it they must understand that of every ten who do, only about one will turn out to have the gift of evangelist and dedicate himself or herself to a structured evangelistic ministry.

So, for those who have been given the gift of evangelist, it is an exciting time of discovery and self-fulfillment. It is a time for them to find just where God expects them to fit into the Body of Christ. In College Hill Presbyterian Church, for example, it is reported that about 200 of the members have become fairly sure they have the gift of evangelist, and 70 of them are currently active in the structured evangelistic outreach program. The 200 represent 10 percent of their membership of approximately 2,000, and the 70 would come out to 3.5 percent. If they were to ask me for advice, I would say to challenge at least another 70 to become active again. That would make 140 in the structured outreach program and probably increase their growth rate from 109 percent to over 200 percent per decade.

And for those who don't have the gift of evangelist, three good things happen. First, they will get rid of any guilt that might build up because they are not as effective in sharing the faith as some other members of the body. They are thereby freed to discover, develop and use to the hilt whatever other gift or gifts God has given them. Second, they will begin to break down the "fear barrier." The fear barrier is one of the most formidable obstacles to effective witness and the training and experience they receive will get rid of it. Third, each member of the church will be a better and more effective witness for Jesus Christ no matter what their gifts are. They will know how to lead a soul to Christ which, in my opinion, is just as important a quality for a balanced Christian life as attending worship, saying grace before meals, giving a tithe and offering to the Lord, or studying the Word of God.

The whole evangelistic tone of the Body of Christ can be improved by understanding how the gift of evangelist functions and putting it into practice. It could be just what your church needs to get the message to the unsaved, bring new believers into your fellowship and begin an exciting era of growth to the glory of God.

Notes

1. Leighton Ford, *Good News Is for Sharing* (Elgin, IL: David C. Cook Publishing Co., 1977), p. 83.
2. *Ibid*.
3. Rick Yohn, *Discover Your Spiritual Gift and Use It* (Wheaton: Tyndale House Publishers, 1974), p. 64.
4. The presence-proclamation-persuasion discussion is further developed in C. Peter Wagner, *Frontiers in Missionary Strategy* (Chicago: Moody Press, 1971), pp. 124-134.
5. Yohn, *Discover Your Spiritual Gift* . . . , p. 64.
6. Ford, *Good News Is for Sharing*, p. 83.
7. David Allan Hubbard, "A Winsome Witness," *Today's Christian* (September, 1976), p. 2.
8. Dean M. Kelley, *Why Conservative Churches Are Growing* (New York: Harper and Row, Publishers, Inc., 1972), recently issued in paperback.

7. Understanding the Missionary Gift

Some books on church growth are written as if the growth of the local church were the only important kind of growth. It certainly is important, it undoubtedly is the kind of growth that pastors of churches and lay leaders are most intensely interested in, and it is obvious that local church growth is emphasized most in this book. But I would not feel that the book was complete if it did not include at least one chapter dealing with the vast number of people outside the normal reach of the evangelistic program of a local church. The spiritual gift that most directly relates to this is the gift of missionary.

Kinds of Church Growth

Church growth theory discerns four basic kinds of growth: *Internal growth is the spiritual growth of Christians who are already members of the Body of Christ.* Through it they learn to love God more deeply, to worship more intensely, to pray more fervently, to witness more effectively, to care for each other more lovingly, to study God's Word more intelligently, and to exhibit other Christian graces that reflect Christian maturity. Internal growth is a prerequisite to other kinds of growth because mature Christians are the instruments God uses for reaching others for Christ and folding them into the fellowship of believers.

Expansion growth is the growth of the local congregation in membership. It is the kind we referred to as the chief concern of most pastors.

Extension growth is growth through planting new churches. Unfortunately, extension growth has been one of the most severely neglected areas for effective evangelism in America. Compared to expansion growth, extension growth is a much more efficient and cost-effective way to evangelize the unchurched even in a "Christian" country like America. I have no doubt in my mind that simply by launching an aggressive program of new church planting, almost any denomination in America could reverse the trends of church membership decline that have been plaguing many of them.

Bridging growth is also growth through planting new churches, but in bridging growth the new churches are planted in a different culture. Extension growth is planting new churches among "our kind of people." Bridging growth is planting churches among another kind of people who could not reasonably be expected to be folded into the fellowship of our church or who simply prefer to worship God in ways different from the way we do it. Bridging growth is (a) the top priority for completing the task of world evangelization, and (b) uniquely dependent on the missionary gift. But before we go into this there is one more set of concepts to explain.

All evangelism is not the same. In the preceding chapter we mentioned the gift of evangelist and the many different variations within which that gift can be exercised. Here are some further variations that bring the cultural aspect into focus:

E-1 evangelism. E-1 evangelism is monocultural. It is the shorthand term that refers to winning those of your own culture to Jesus Christ and assumes that they will feel at home in your own kind of local church. It includes both expansion and extension growth.

E-2 and E-3 evangelism. Both E-2 and E-3 are cross-cultural. They are actually subdivisions of bridging growth. E-2 is evangelization in cultures different from the culture of the evangelist, but only slightly different. E-3 is evangelism in vastly different cultures. The difference between the two is in degree, not in kind, since they both involve starting churches in different cultures. Note that geographical distances have nothing to do with this. People at an E-3 distance can often be found in the same city.

E-0 evangelism. To complete the picture, E-0 evangelism means winning people to Christ who are already church members. Some churches in America have large numbers of members who are not born again or committed to Christ, people who obviously need to be evangelized.

The "Hidden People"

This is a book on church growth. Most of the content is on E-1 *expansion* growth. But this chapter focuses on E-2 and E-3 *bridging* growth. Thus it addresses itself to the challenge of the "hidden people," those thousands of millions of people in the world who have not yet heard of Jesus Christ and who need someone from outside their own culture to bring them the good news. This chapter also pulls into focus the vast numbers of ethnics in America who in many cases are in need of an E-2 or E-3 witness from the majority Anglo-American churches.

Those interested in the total fulfillment of the Great Commission need to see the whole picture. No one has done more consistent and thorough research on this than Ralph Winter of the U.S. Center for World Mission. He addressed the 1974 International Congress on World Evangelization at Lausanne, Switzerland, on the subject "The Highest Priority: Cross-Cultural Evangelism,"[1] bringing world attention to this tremendous need. His center, while admitting the need for E-0 and E-1 evangelism, nevertheless has dedicated all its resources to E-2 and E-3. From Winter we learn that, for the purposes of evangelization, the world can be divided statistically into four categories:[2]

Active Christians are people who have been truly born again or committed to Christ. These people are responsible members of local churches, who believe the Bible and who take seriously its command to make disciples of all nations. Of a total of 4,123 million people in the world, there are an estimated 222 million active Christians.

Inactive Christians would answer "Christian" if asked what their religion is on a world census. But most of them are Christian in name only. Not that many of them might not be accepted by God into His family, but in any case they are not turned on by sharing their faith in any way with others. They provide little hope for evangelization. It is estimated that they number 1,023 million. Adding the active Christians to them, we get a total figure of 1,245 million Christians, active and inactive, in the world. This is something like 30 percent of the world's population.

Culturally-near non-Christians do not yet know Jesus Christ. But their culture has a viable Christian church and they can likely be reached by E-1 evangelism. Sometimes they might be quite far removed from other Christians of their own kind of people *geographically*, but culturally they are near neighbors. They number approximately 467 million.

Culturally-distant non-Christians are people who are part of a culture into which Christianity has not yet penetrated. They are the "hidden people." The only way they can be reached is by E-2 and E-3 cross-cultural evangelism. The most surprising thing about them is not so much that they are there, but that there are so many of them. An astonishing 2,411 million of the world's population are hidden people. This figures out to be 59 percent of the world. There are many more hidden people than there are Christans. Little wonder that they are considered the highest priority.

The most difficult kind of evangelism is E-3, and the second most difficult is E-2. E-1 extension growth (starting new churches in the same culture) is the next most difficult and E-1 expansion is the easiest. This is one reason that, unless a special point is made of it, E-1 tends to take the front seat and E-2/E-3 become some item quite far down the agenda.

The greatest challenge for cross-cultural evangelism is, of course, what we usually think of as the foreign mission field. The largest numbers of hidden people are found among Chinese, Hindus, and Muslims in that order. But this should not blind us to the great need for E-2 and E-3 evangelistic work right here in America.

"People-Blindness" and Its Cure

Many do not recognize hidden people because of "people-blindness." People-blindness is the malady that prevents us from seeing groups of people around us who are not able to hear the message of the gospel or respond to it in the ways that we tend to express it. Those with people-blindness think that their church is good enough for everyone and their doors are open to all. If some people do not like what they find there it is their problem, not ours. They feel that all Christians should talk alike, worship alike, enjoy the same kind of music, have their services at the same time and the same length, and form close friendships with people from many different kinds of groups.

The fact of the matter is that churches don't grow that way. Throughout history, Christian churches have normally grown among just one kind of people through E-1 evangelism. Congregational life is attractive to unbelievers when they see people in those congregations that they know and they can feel at home with. If they can't feel at home, they will best be won to Christ through E-2 or E-3 evangelism. That means starting new churches that from the beginning will be *their* kind of churches, not *our* kind of churches. All foreign missionaries know this principle of church growth, but some Americans find it harder to apply in their own country. They suffer from people-blindness partially as a result of their embarrassment over racism, discrimination and social injustices that have been perpetrated in America by the dominant Anglo-Americans.

Throughout history the ethnics in America have been such a nuisance that we Anglos have tried to solve the problem through assimilation. Under the slogan of "melting pot," the general idea has been that the best ethnics are those who most nearly conform to our Anglo-American culture. "America, love it or leave it," has been a slogan to try to make other people self-conscious about talking Spanish or black English or with a foreign accent. In America, non-Anglos have been considered "culturally disadvantaged." We want them all to be like us. We feel that one way to speed up this process is to make them come to our churches. To encourage them to have their own churches is unthinkable to a person with people-blindness who perpetuates the "melting pot" theory.

Fortunately for evangelism and church growth, the assimilationist model for understanding American society is giving way to a more open-minded concept since the civil rights movement of the sixties taught us that "black is beautiful." As a result, E-2 and E-3 evangelism is becoming a much more acceptable challenge for American Christians.[3]

The first mainline denomination to understand this and to concentrate heavily on the principles of E-2 and E-3 evangelism was the Southern Baptists. Their Home Mission Board in Atlanta, particularly under the leadership of Wendell Belew, director of the Missions Ministries Division and Oscar Romo, director of the Language Missions Department, which specializes in cross-cultural evangelism, has led the way. Today Southern Baptists are probably five to ten years ahead of most other denominations in perceiving the true spiritual need of Americans who are "unmelted," so to speak, and in planting among them something different from the ordinary Southern Baptist Anglo-American church.

Their results are phenomenal. Already there are over 2,000 Southern Baptist churches among 35 different major ethnic groups in America, not counting many of the subgroups such as different Indian tribes. The largest Southern Baptist church in California, for example, is Chinese. The largest one in New England is Haitian French and the second largest is Arab. There are more

Southern Baptist Arab congregations meeting in the United States than in all the Arab countries put together. If all the Southern Baptist Spanish language congregations in the United States were to form one convention, it would be larger than any other Spanish language convention in the world. There are more Southern Baptist Vietnamese congregations in America now than there were in Vietnam when it fell to the Communists in 1974. Since January of 1971, a new Korean Southern Baptist church has been started every month of the year. Every month now sees two new Chinese works and two new Laotian works.

Oscar Romo maintains that all churches, like it or not, are cultural, ethnic or subculture groupings. He philosophizes, "Our job is to evangelize, not to assimilate. People go to church because they want to. If they don't want to, they won't go. You go where you feel comfortable."[4]

Recognizing the need for cross-cultural sensitivity among Christians, he goes on to say, "To reach people, we must be aware of cultural units and cultural differences. There has to be room for the gospel to penetrate a given group without necessarily changing that group's background. It changes their sense of values, but you still end up having subcultures."[5]

Southern Baptists exhibit the cure for "people-blindness." It is a frank and honest recognition that peoplehood and culture have their own integrity and that the communication of the gospel does not require that these important human characteristics be violated. This is the main reason why Southern Baptists are so far ahead of all other basically Anglo denominations in their effective evangelistic efforts among non-Anglos in the United States. Other denominations that feel they should also be ministering to the minority groups in

America will have to learn how to do E-2 and E-3 evangelism. Many are now frustrated because they are trying to do cross-cultural evangelism by using E-1 methods. They might as well try to swim in a suit of medieval armor.

How the Gospel Spreads

The most important incidents for the spread of the gospel in the New Testament after Jesus' ascension were (a) the jump from Hebrew Jews to Hellenistic Jews (see Acts 2), (b) the jump from Jews to Samaritans (see Acts 8) and (c) the jump from Jews to Gentiles (see Acts 11). They were all cross-cultural E-2 and E-3 situations.

This is true today also. The most significant events in world evangelization occur when the gospel takes permanent root in a new culture, among a hidden people.

I need to repeat, most individuals, perhaps 98 percent are won to Christ through E-1 evangelism, by their own kind of people. Although we do not yet have hard data to substantiate this figure, if it is reasonably accurate we could also say categorically that the winning of the 2 percent who need to be won by E-2 and E-3 evangelism constitutes the most important challenge for world evangelization today. It is like the Viking mission sent by NASA to explore the surface of Mars. The Viking spacecraft that lands on the surface transmits television pictures and analyzes soil samples, does most of the scientific work. But it is there only because of the launching rockets that first set it in motion through space. After the launching systems do their job, they disappear. E-2 and E-3 evangelism is the launching rocket for world evangelization. When its job is done, E-1 takes over and the evangelistic process continues without much need for the missionaries. One more people has been reached.

Cross-cultural evangelism is not a modern invention. It did not even start with William Carey, although E-2 and E-3 evangelism were never as potent as they have been since William Carey began the modern missionary movement almost two centuries ago. This has been the way the gospel has spread since the day of Pentecost. It is the way most of our own ancestors originally heard and received the gospel. With 2.4 billion hidden people still on planet Earth, cross-cultural evangelism remains the highest priority for the Body of Christ if Christ's command to "make disciples of all nations [peoples]" is to be taken seriously.

One of the most important and encouraging phenomena of contemporary Christianity is the awakening of churches in the Third World to their responsibility for E-2 and E-3 evangelism. Up to recently, most of the cross-cultural work has been undertaken by the European and American churches. The majority of missionaries are still white, but the number of red, black, yellow and brown missionaries is rapidly increasing.[6] If this trend continues, which it undoubtedly will, more and more of the world's hidden peoples will be reached in our generation.

Gift 25: The Gift of Missionary

The success of E-2 and E-3 evangelization, necessary to reach the 2.4 billion hidden people of the world, is uniquely dependent upon the spiritual gift of missionary. This is a hidden gift for hidden people. I say hidden gift, because hardly any book on spiritual gifts discusses it or even acknowledges it as a gift. One reason for this might be that it is not as explicitly described as a spiritual gift in the Bible as most of the others, although it appears in a biblical passage that is clear enough once it is explained.

The gift of missionary is the special ability that God gives to some members of the Body of Christ to minister whatever other spiritual gifts they have in a second culture.

Most Christians, as most human beings, are monocultural. They are born and raised and die among only one kind of people. Their culture enables them to interact with and behave like and understand others around them without any special training other than the process of socialization which we all go through at an early age. They may, of course, come into contact with other cultures from time to time. They may travel abroad and enjoy seeing other kinds of people. They may live in a city in America where housing and schools and employment are integrated and where contact with people from other cultures is part of daily life. They may even have close friends with people from another culture. They may have gone so far as to learn a foreign language. All this, and most people still are monocultural.

People with the gift of missionary not only enjoy coming into contact with other cultures, they go through a second process of socialization called "acculturation." They enjoy the challenge of living in another culture while cutting ties with their first culture on a long-term basis. When they do, they get culture shock, but they recover rapidly. They may be attacked by "Montezuma's Revenge" but they eventually become immune to the new bugs in the food and drink of another people. They learn the language more rapidly than those without the gift. They quickly pick up slang words, tones of voice, and body language not described in textbooks. They feel at home with people of the second culture. And, most of all, they are eventually accepted by the others as "one of us."

While intercultural contact is enriching for every person, God does not expect every Christian to identify with a second culture. He gives the gift of missionary only to some. To how many. I don't know. I have said 5 percent in the past, but this now seems a little high to me. In the United States, out of about 50 million active Christian adults, some 40,000 are serving as missionaries. This is less than one-tenth of one percent! Perhaps the ideal figure is not as high as 5 percent, but still there must be thousands of Christians in America to whom God has given the gift of missionary who have not yet discovered it and who are not using it. With 2.4 billion hidden people in the world and masses of unevangelized ethnics here in the United States, certainly to double or triple the number of American missionaries would not be an unreasonable goal.

Projecting the Gift of Missionary

The gift of missionary is another one of those gifts that is frequently projected. Time and again I hear some enthusiastic preacher say, "Every Christian is a missionary!" The doctrine of spiritual gifts tells us that this is a ridiculous statement. In most cases, however, I do not think they are referring to specialized E-2 and E-3 evangelism. They probably have never realized that there is such a thing as a missionary gift. What they probably are trying to say is "Every Christian is a witness," and with that I heartily concur.

In a way it is counterproductive to encourage anyone at all to volunteer to be a cross-cultural missionary. Sad to say, there are some missionaries who have been on the field for 30 years who never had the gift in the first place. Both their home church and the mission field would have been better off if they had stayed home. The mission field is something like the Marine Corps: God needs a few choice (gifted) men and women. If there is any place in God's work for a high degree of aptitude, training and competence, it is in the cross-cultural task of reaching the hidden people. I don't believe it is helpful to give an appeal at a missionary conference that says, "You must go to the field unless God calls you to stay home!" It is better to focus the appeal on discovering spiritual gifts.

Sometimes the gift of missionary is confused with the gift of evangelist. It should be evident, however, that some evangelists have the missionary gift and some don't. Those who do should evangelize in another culture (as well as in their own), but those who don't should concentrate on a monocultural ministry. They will be effective in E-1 evangelism, but not in the trickier E-2 and E-3 evangelism.

Another major area of confusion that often arises is between the missionary and the apostle. Before we contrast the two let's first take a look at the gift of apostle.

Gift 16: The Gift of Apostle

Although I am a strong supporter of *The Living Bible*, I regret that it frequently translates the Greek *apostolos* (apostle) as "missionary." This tends to cloud the important distinction between the gift of missionary and the gift of apostle.

The biblical evidence strongly supports the continuity of the gift of apostle. The original 12 apostles have a unique place in Christian history and they will be commemorated permanently in the New Jerusalem (see Rev. 21:14), but they were not the only apostles. First Corinthians 15 mentions that after the resurrection Jesus appeared to "the twelve" and then also to "all the apostles," indicating that there were apostles other than the twelve (1 Cor. 15:5,7). Furthermore the warnings against "false apostles" would be nonsense if apostles were limited to the twelve (see 2 Cor. 11:13; Rev. 2:2).

Several, other than the Twelve, are mentioned by name as apostles. They include Matthias (see Acts 1: 26), Paul (see Rom. 1:1), Barnabas (see Acts 14:14) Andronicus and Junias (see Rom. 16:7), Timothy and Silas (see 1 Thess. 2:6). Through the ages as well as today, many of God's gifted servants have been and are true apostles.

The gift of apostle is the special ability that God gives to certain members of the Body of Christ which enables them to assume and exercise general leadership over a number of churches with an extraordinary authority in spiritual matters that is spontaneously recognized and appreciated by those churches.

The apostle is the person whom God has given especially to pastors and church leaders. He is the one to whom pastors and church leaders can go for counsel and help. He is a peacemaker, a troubleshooter and a problem solver. He can make demands that may sound autocratic but which are gladly accepted by Christian people because they recognize his gift and the authority it carries with it. He has the overall picture in focus and is not restricted in vision to the problems of one local church.

Today there are many titles given to those who are assigned responsibility over a number of churches. Depending on the denomination they can be called bishops, district superintendents, overseers, moderators, conference ministers, presidents, executive secretaries, and perhaps other titles. All of these should be selected because their spiritual gift of apostle has been recognized by the Body as a whole. It is no secret, however, that many, if not most, are elevated to their position on the basis of seniority, prestige, personality or politics. This soon becomes evident by the kind of leadership mode they assume. To borrow sociological terms, these leaders may fall into one of two kinds of leadership categories:

Rational-legal leadership—their authority comes from their position, not from their person. They are obeyed, sometimes grudgingly, because of the office they represent, not because of their gift. They are often gloomy, irascible, pessimistic and frustrated. They are easily threatened by up-and-coming leadership.

Charismatic leadership—their authority is derived from a God-given gift. Others obey them because they want to and have great confidence in their counsel. Their leadership does not depend on the office, although the office is important. They are usually easy-going, unthreatened, optimistic, and pleasant to be around. I believe this is God's mode for apostolic leadership.

I frankly hope this discussion will cause some presently in office to reexamine themselves and resign. The prestige and status that such ecclesiastical positions carry is not worth the personal frustration of trying to minister without a gift and the ultimate harm it does to the Body of Christ. It is always best to think soberly of oneself (see Rom. 12:3). Vacancies caused by such resignations should be filled strictly with people whose gift of apostle has been recognized.

One of the ways the gift of apostle is most readily recognized is for the apostle to start new churches. In many cases this has happened, beginning with the apostle Paul. Paul combined the gift of evangelist (the church-planting variety) with the gift of apostle. This is a frequently hyphenated gift.

Contemporary Apostles

Pastor Chuck Smith of Calvary Chapel, Costa Mesa, California, is an example of a contemporary apostle. He is the senior minister of Calvary Chapel, the mother church which he founded (to all intents and purposes) during the Jesus People Movement of the late sixties. This local church itself ministers to upwards of 25,000 people every week and is growing at a decadal rate of about 4,000 percent—probably the largest and fastest growing church in America.

Not only is Chuck Smith the pastor of the mother church, but his leadership has encouraged at least 80 other Calvary Chapel churches to be planted throughout the country. Most of them are in Southern California, but others are as far away as Pennsylvania, Arkansas, Colorado and Oregon. Within another decade, I would not be surprised if Calvary Chapels were found in most of the 50 states with a cumulative membership of over one million. As an example of rapid church growth in today's America, Calvary Chapel can hardly be surpassed.

Although he might well deny it, this growth is due substantially to the apostolic gift that God has given to Chuck Smith just as surely as the growth of the churches in first century Asia Minor were due to Paul's apostolic gift. Chuck Smith well fits the kind of charismatic leadership pattern suggested above. A recent newspaper story on Calvary Chapel describes him as "age 51, a balding, ebullient Bible teacher who radiates good health and friendly, open cheerfulness which attracts crowds of enthusiastic believers and followers."[7] But this is not the whole picture. I am told that among peers in the leadership positions in the various Calvary Chapels, Chuck Smith's "soft" words carry incredible authority. When he speaks what he feels to be God's will he says it quietly, he says it only once, and he expects it to be obeyed. It usually is.

There are other apostles like this: Manoel de Melo in Sao Paulo, Brazil; Javier Vasquez in Santiago, Chile;

Cho Yonggi in Seoul, Korea; Robert Hymers of Westwood, California. I am certain enough of these four to mention them in print. Undoubtedly there are hundreds of others worldwide who should be recognized as such. This in turn might allow yet other hundreds to discover that they have the gift of apostle and see it confirmed by the Body of Christ. If they follow the lead of the contemporary apostles I have mentioned, incredible church growth will result.

The Gift of Missionary in the Bible

Paul not only had the gifts of apostle and evangelist, but he also had the gift of missionary. He was a cross-cultural worker and constantly perceived himself in that role. Ephesians 3 is the chapter on the gift of missionary. There Paul speaks of his special ability, as a Jew, to carry the gospel to the Gentiles. Paul was "a Pharisee, the son of a Pharisee" (Acts 23:6), a Hebrew "brought up . . . at the feet of Gamaliel" (Acts 22:3), and a recipient of the legacy of prejudice and disdain that all Jews had for Gentiles in the first century. One commentator speculated that the only prejudice barrier in today's world that even approaches the feeling of first century Jews for Gentiles is the prejudice that Brahmins have for untouchables in India. For a Jew to reach Gentiles effectively, supernatural help was definitely needed.

Paul says that his ability to communicate to Gentiles that they should be members of the Body of Christ just like Jews was due to the "gift of the grace" that God gave him (Eph. 3:7). This is a clear reference to a spiritual gift which I have chosen to call the gift of missionary, even though that label itself is not so stated in the Bible. But if Paul's gift was cross-cultural communication, which is indicated here, "missionary" seems to fit the concept well.

In each one of the three accounts of Paul's conversion in the book of Acts, this gift is mentioned. For example, Ananias of Damascus, the man God used to speak to Paul and restore his sight after his experience on the Damascus Road, heard these words about Paul from God Himself: "He is a chosen vessel unto me, to bear my name before the Gentiles" (Acts 9:15). So consistently did Paul live out his specific calling to minister to the Gentiles that not only did he defend their point of view in the Jerusalem Council (see Acts 15), but he ultimately was arrested and imprisoned because the Jews thought he had gone so far as to turn traitor and betray them (see Acts 21:28,29).

Paul, in 1 Corinthians 9, described what the missionary gift looked like to him. He mentioned that he could become a Jew to Jews and a Gentile ("without law") to the Gentiles. "I am made all things to all men," he said, "that I might by all means save some" (1 Cor. 9:22). Successful cross-cultural workers today exhibit the same qualities. It is relatively easy for them to do it because God enables them with the gift of missionary.

Paul and Peter

Both Paul and Peter had the gift of apostle and were so recognized by the churches. But Paul also had the gift of missionary and Peter did not. Paul was a cross-cultural apostle and Peter was a monocultural apostle. Peter, it is true, had some cross-cultural experiences. He was chosen to present the gospel to the Gentiles in the house of Cornelius and it was an extremely difficult experience for him. He later visited the Gentile churches in Antioch, but when the crunch came he refused to eat with Gentiles and infuriated his friend Paul. Paul had to relate in the Epistle to the Galatians how he withstood Peter to his face in Antioch (see Gal.

2:11), and he once and for all clarified that he was an apostle to the uncircumcision (Gentiles) while Peter was an apostle to the circumcision (Jews) (see Gal. 2:7,8). Peter had a hard time in cross-cultural situations mainly because he did not have the same gift Paul had.

Not only Peter, but James and John also recognized that they were apostles without the missionary gift. This is described in Galatians 2:9 where James, Peter and John recognize that Paul had a special "grace" (the root word for *charisma* is used here), and that thereby, Paul and Barnabas should do the cross-cultural work among Gentiles while the other three remained in monocultural work among Jews.

Some may not like this term "gift of missionary." It matters little to me what the function is called. By whatever name, we need a continually growing army of men and women who have whatever spiritual gift or gifts are necessary to reach 2.4 billion hidden people in our generation. This is my greatest burden, and I believe it is in tune with the burden of God Himself.

The Role of "World Christian"

While only a few have the gift of missionary and thereby are expected to minister in a second culture, all Christians have a role of supporting God's program to "make disciples of all nations" (see Matt. 28:19) in every way possible. I like the term now being used to designate people who in one way or another have become informed about the cause of world missions and who are participating in whatever way they can. The exercise of their role is above average. They are called "World Christians." World Christians may have a variety of other spiritual gifts, but they have decided to use their gifts in a way that specifically furthers the cause of reaching the hidden people.

Donald Hamilton, for example, has the gift of administration. He knows how to plan, how to run a smooth office, how to manage a staff, how to relate well to others, how to promote his "product." For years he exhibited this as a natural talent with the Xerox Corporation. But he knew his administrative ability was also a spiritual gift, so he resigned his position with Xerox and later became the founder and director of the Association of Church Missions Committees (ACMC). He is my model of a World Christian. He eats, drinks and sleeps missions. He knows the world. He knows missiological theory. He is not a cross-cultural person with the gift of missionary, but few people with the missionary gift are making the widespread contribution to the total missionary task of the church as Donald Hamilton with his gift of administration.

The ACMC has given a dignity and sense of cohesion to the missionary committees of over 300 churches of all denominations. If we can assume that each committee includes eight lay-people, Hamilton is then working with some 2,400 church members who are already World Christians or becoming that way. The ACMC is also in constant touch with the missionary agencies, both denominational and interdenominational. It insists on high standards in the kind of reporting an agency does to its constituency as to philosophy of missions, financial policies, monitoring of personnel, and goal accomplishment.[8]

Training for World Christians is now being developed to a very high degree by the U.S. Center for World Mission under the direction of Ralph Winter. Winter was burdened when he discovered that Inter-Varsity Christian Fellowship had not developed ongoing programs to give special training in missions to the thousands of college students who signed commitment cards for missions at the triennial Urbana missionary conventions. He then established the Institute for International Studies which allows students from any university to take credit-bearing courses designed to give them special insights into contemporary missions. Hundreds of college students have taken these courses and, through them, many have begun the process of discovering that they have been given the missionary gift. Those who find they do not have the gift end up making their contribution as lifetime World Christians.[9]

A special correspondence course has also been developed for those who would like to get training that will help them become World Christians, but who cannot attend formal classes. Called "Crucial Dimensions of World Evangelization," it is also available through the U.S. Center for World Mission either for credit or non-credit. Contributors to the course include Ralph Winter, Paul Hiebert, Arthur Glasser, and myself.[10]

Experimenting with the missionary gift is more possible today than ever before. Increasing numbers of the missionary force of North American missionaries are short-term workers who sign up for a few months to a few years for some specialized job. If these short-term workers do this in prayer and with the expectation that, through the experience, God will indicate clearly if this is a gift and if cross-cultural work should become a career, it can be one of the most creative experiences of your life. Intercristo of Seattle, Washington is recognized as a clearinghouse for information on short-term missionary service.[11]

Whether through the gift of missionary or the role of World Christian, Christian resources, as never before, need to be poured out on behalf of the 2.4 billion hidden people of the world. I suppose that if I had to name my strongest personal desire for this book on spiritual gifts, it would have to be right here in helping to mobilize Christians for this crucial aspect of world evangelization. I have a strong hunch that it would be God's desire also.

Notes

1. Ralph D. Winter, "The Highest Priority: Cross-Cultural Evangelism," *Let the Earth Hear His Voice*, J.D. Douglas, ed. (Minneapolis: World Wide Publications, 1975).
2. The data used in this chapter are taken from a pamphlet by Ralph D. Winter, "Penetrating the Last Frontiers" (Pasadena: U.S. Center for World Mission, 1978). It is also included as a chapter in Edward R. Dayton and C. Peter Wagner, eds., *Unreached Peoples 1979* (Elgin, Illinois: David C. Cook, 1978).
3. For a detailed discussion of this see C. Peter Wagner, *Our Kind of People* (Atlanta: John Knox Press, 1978).
4. Romo is quoted in Dan Martin, "The Church-Growth Questions," *Home Missions* (December, 1977), p. 19.
5. *Ibid*.
6. Those who wish more information on the rising tide of missions from Asian, African and Latin American churches should read Marlin L. Nelson's two books, *The How and Why of Third World Missions* and *Readings in Third World Missions* (Pasadena: William Carey Library, 1976).
7. George Grey, "Calvary Chapels Sprouting Like Mushrooms Over U.S.," *The Register* (March 26, 1978), p. 1.
8. For further information about the Association of Church Missions Committees, write Donald A. Hamilton, Executive Secretary, 1021 E. Walnut Street, Suite 202, Pasadena, California 91106.
9. For further information on the Institute for International Studies, write Ralph D. Winter, President, U.S. Center for World Mission, 1605 E. Elizabeth Street, Pasadena, California 91104.
10. Information on the correspondence course can be obtained from the above address.
11. The address of Intercristo is Box 9323, Seattle, Washington 98109.

8. The Rest of the Body

Up to this point 17 spiritual gifts have been defined and discussed. Of them, the primary gift for total world evangelization was identified as the gift of missionary. The primary gift for local church growth is the gift of evangelist. The primary gift for the total health of the local church is the gift of pastor. These three gifts, pastor, evangelist and missionary are so crucial for church growth that each was given a whole chapter. The other 14 were brought up as they related to the three major gifts or as they illustrated some general principle of spiritual gifts.

In this chapter the remaining 10 gifts will be defined and discussed. I need to state once again that they are not secondary to the health of the Body of Christ any more than the ears and the tongue and the lungs and the skin are secondary to bodily health in general. But they are secondary to the reproductive function in both cases. Therefore, because this book is concentrating on the relationship of spiritual gifts and church growth, these 10 gifts will be discussed more briefly than some of the others.

Furthermore, I have chosen to group them in four clusters of gifts which appear to have a relationship to one another.

Gift 9: The Gift of Knowledge

Although the twin gifts of wisdom and knowledge are mentioned in that order in 1 Corinthians 12, I am reversing the order here because I want to discuss them in sequence. Knowledge has to do with the discovery of truth while wisdom has to do with its application to life.

The gift of knowledge is the special ability that God gives to certain members of the Body of Christ to discover, accumulate, analyze and clarify information and ideas that are pertinent to the growth and well-being of the body.

It is frequently pointed out that the Greek term for this gift is two words, sometimes translated "word of knowledge." It could also be translated "the ability to speak with knowledge." The person with this gift is a lead learner. He is expected to get the truth first and to originate new ideas. He is eager to learn, has a long attention span, and is able to absorb and retain unusual amounts of information. He is a scholar, at home with research, and is often found in the academic world. Unless he has other gifts that counteract this, the person with the gift of knowledge usually has a low need for people. He or she is more comfortable with ideas than with individuals. Gossiping is not one of this person's temptations— in fact it bores him or her terribly.

Sometimes the gift of teaching is associated with the gift of knowledge, so the person becomes a scholar-teacher, which happens to be my own dominant gift-mix. But sometimes the gift of teacher is not added to the gift of knowledge. Pure scholars have vast amounts of knowledge, have the ability to figure out intricate relationships between ideas, are wizards at solving intellectual problems, but have little feeling for the needs of a given audience. In a classroom they tend to be boring and irrelevant, and few people learn anything from them unless they happen to be fellow scholars in precisely the same field.

On the other hand, scholar-teachers might not have quite the intellectual capacities as the pure scholar because much of their energy is invested in working out ways and means to present effectively the knowledge they have accumulated. They have an intuition that tells them what to include in a lecture and what to leave out. They know how to pause, how to use body language, how to vary the voice, how to make use of visuals of one kind or another. They have a sense of timing as to when to introduce a new idea or concept. They know how to stimulate and guide discussion. They have a feeling as to when discussion is helping the class or when it is becoming irrelevant; then they cut it off at the right moment.

People with the gift of knowledge cannot explain where their ideas come from. When they need them, the ideas are simply there, or they soon will be. But these people need time by themselves for idea development, which may explain why those with the gift of knowledge seem to be bugged by too many people. Seminary professors frequently joke with one another by saying, "This would be a great place if it just weren't for the students!" That is why, as I have explained, I like to be left alone on a long airplane flight. At 35,000 feet ideas seem to come to me in unusual volume.

Some of those with the gift of knowledge who are making a very direct contribution to the spread of the gospel are Bible translators. Wycliffe, the Lutheran Bible Translators, and the several Bible societies around the world recruit translators with the gift of knowledge, often combined with the gift of missionary. The hours and hours of patient search for words and concepts in an unwritten language take incredible concentration. Because they have the gift, translators love their agony and isolation, a kind of joy that few others in the Body can personally identify with. Most Christians are glad someone is translating the Bible in hundreds of remote jungle villages, but they are glad it is someone else. Together they praise God for spiritual gifts!

Gift 8: The Gift of Wisdom

I like Ralph Neighbour's analogy of the medical model to explain the difference between the gift of knowledge and the gift of wisdom.[1] The person with the gift of knowledge does spiritual things like the medical researcher who gets new insights into physiology, genetics, or vaccines. The person with the gift of wisdom is like the physician who has the ability to diagnose the patient's problem and apply the resources of medical science to that particular case.

The gift of wisdom is the special ability that God gives to certain members of the Body of Christ to know the mind of the Holy Spirit in such a way as to receive insight into how given knowledge may best be applied to specific needs arising in the Body of Christ.

The person with the gift of wisdom knows how to get to the heart of a problem quickly. He or she has a practical mind and is a problem solver. He or she has little difficulty in making decisions because that person can predict with a high degree of accuracy what the outcome of the decisions will be. When a person with the gift of wisdom speaks, other members of the Body recognize that truth has been spoken and the right course of action recommended. Formal learning is not at all a prerequisite. Long hours of digging out new facts may not appeal at all to the person with the gift of wisdom.

One of my good friends with the gift of wisdom is Leighton Ford. I have already stated that he has the gift of evangelist, but there is another gift in his mix. I have observed Leighton Ford closely as the chairman of the Lausanne Committee on World Evangelization, particularly in the executive committee where most of the tough decisions need to be made. The executive committee is a motley group of high-powered individuals who have strong opinions on almost every issue imaginable. I have found myself in the midst of discussions where the points of view have been so divergent that there seemed to be no human way of reconciling them.

But Ford has the unusual ability to stay above the give and take, not to get involved in the emotions of the discussion, and just at the right time to come up with a suggestion for action which sounds exactly right to the other members of the committee. The gift of wisdom provides him with a sensitivity as to what each person is trying to say, to what extent he or she is willing to compromise, and what are the particular personal needs each one has at the moment. His gift is confirmed by a feeling on the part of all members that their point of view has been adequately heard and fairly considered. The result is both individual satisfaction and group harmony.

Since I spend most of my time in the field of church

growth, I continue to observe how God distributes gifts among my colleagues. Those who are functioning successfully as church diagnosticians and consultants have the gift of wisdom, it seems to me. I stand amazed at the insight and perception that consultants like John Wimber and Lyle Schaller and Carl George have when called upon to help solve the growth problems of a particular church. I am amazed because I myself have tried it enough to know that I am not very good at it at all.

I seem to be at my best developing new hypotheses from information I gather from books and from being out in the field talking to church leaders and observing growing churches. Then I present it in the classroom, usually to professional ministers, receive the feedback from them that causes me to revise the original hypotheses, then put the results in a book. This, I believe, is the gift of knowledge.

But when it comes to sitting down with Reverend So-and-so who wants to know what to do in his own parish with all these theories I have fed him, I am in trouble. That's one reason I established a Church Growth Department in Fuller Evangelistic Association and invited practitioners with the gift of wisdom like John Wimber and Carl George to join me in the venture. That, as I understand it, is the way the Body of Christ is supposed to function.

The Gifts of Mercy, Helps and Service

More research needs to be done on this, but on the surface it appears to me that the gifts of mercy, helps, and service are high-percentage gifts. While they are high percentage they are also low visibility. These are gifts which do not attract much attention or much publicity. Few people become famous for helping others. For every apostle or evangelist or prophet, probably 10 people with mercy, helps and service are needed to keep the whole Body healthy.

Gift 7: The Gift of Mercy

The gift of mercy is the special ability that God gives to certain members of the Body of Christ to feel genuine empathy and compassion for individuals, both Christian and non-Christian, who suffer distressing physical, mental or emotional problems, and to translate that compassion into cheerfully-done deeds that reflect Christ's love and alleviate the suffering.

Those with the gift of mercy engage in one-on-one relationships. They seek out those who need help and develop a personal ministry with them. They show a practical, compassionate love. Kindness comes naturally, and expects no repayment. While the gift of exhortation helps people mainly with *words* of love, the gift of mercy helps people mainly through *deeds* of love.

The recipients of the gift of mercy are the ill, the retarded, the prisoners, the blind, the poor, the aged, the ugly, the handicapped, the shut-ins, the mentally ill. The gift is directed to both believers and unbelievers. It involves giving a cup of cold water in the name of Jesus.

Every Christian is expected to be merciful. This is a role that reflects the fruit of the Spirit. But those with the gift of mercy make compassion and kindness their life-style. They do not simply react to emergencies, as every Christian is supposed to do. They continually seek opportunities to show pity for the miserable.

Although I haven't visited there in some time, the First Baptist Church of Hammond, Indiana has mobilized its members with the gift of mercy as few others. I am deeply impressed with the ministry to the handicapped which they have developed. The last time I was there I saw 450 "educable slows" receiving patient and compassionate care and teaching from wonderful saints of God whose names may never make the headlines like their pastor, Jack Hyles. I saw buses with hydraulic lifts to accommodate wheelchairs—a sizable investment of funds which cannot be expected to come back in the offering plate from those who use the buses. Added to this are growing programs for the deaf and the blind. This is one reason the church has been maintaining a decadal growth rate of over 400 percent.

Gift 17: The Gift of Helps

By sheer coincidence I am writing this chapter during National Secretaries' Week. While I am thankful for my gifts, I fully realize that without the help of a secretary, my gifts would instantly drop to less than 50 percent effectiveness. The fruitful exercise of my gifts is highly dependent on the gift of helps.

The gift of helps is the special ability that God gives to some members of the Body of Christ to invest the talents they have in the life and ministry of other members of the Body, thus enabling the person helped to increase the effectiveness of his or her spiritual gifts.

Raymond Ortlund once described people with the gift of helps as "the glorious company of the stretcher-bearers." He referred to a person with the gift as "the fourth man with the stretcher"—the stretcher taking the paralyzed man to Jesus in Mark 2:1-12. Whoever heard his name? Who has ever heard the names of Inez Smith or Leola Linkous or Stephanie Wills or Marge Kelley or Irma Griswold? They are all exercising their gift of helps as secretaries or administrative assistants. The names of the persons they help, however, have become household words through the spiritual gifts their secretaries make more effective. The women mentioned are investing their lives to help David Hubbard, Leighton Ford, Billy

Graham, Robert Schuller and Bill Bright respectively.

Like the gift of mercy, the gift of helps is usually a one-on-one ministry. Unlike the gift of mercy, however, the recipients of the benefits are not ordinarily the down and out but other Christians exercising their gifts.

Two varieties of the gift of helps impress me tremendously. One is editors. I find myself to be a terrible editor. I hate working on other people's material. Graduate students who select me as a mentor know that they are largely on their own for their theses or dissertations. Other faculty members, however, seem to have the gift of helps and they will spend hours editing and rewriting for the student. Books like this one are greatly improved between the manuscript and the printed page by the editors whom the publishers assign to polish the work. I am ever so grateful to people who do this kind of work.

The ultimate example of people with the gift of helps has to be ghost writers. Some Christian celebrities produce books and sermons largely written by other people who never so much as get their name in a by-line. It must be because it is so foreign to my own gift-mix that I have developed so much admiration for someone to whom God gives a gift to do such a wonderful thing for other people.

When spiritual gifts are mobilized in any given local church, a large percentage of people will undoubtedly find that their gift is the gift of helps. And what a relief they will be to many a pastor who is overworked by a hundred jobs which have little to do with ministering his own spiritual gifts.

Gift 2: The Gift of Service

Many versions translate the Greek word for this gift as "ministry," which is literally correct. But since "minister" is a rather technical word in our contemporary religious language here in America, I think it is less confusing to call it service. In most cases this gift has little to do with the person who functions as the professional minister of a church.

Actually, the Greek *diakonos* (minister or servant) is our word for deacon. In some churches, however, the job descriptions of deacons require gifts other than just the gift of service. Originally, however, a deacon was simply one who served others.

The gift of service is the special ability that God gives to certain members of the Body of Christ to idenify the unmet needs involved in a task related to God's work, and to make use of available resources to meet those needs and help accomplish the desired goals.

The gift of service is not a one-on-one, person-centered gift like the gifts of mercy and helps. It is more task-oriented. The service is usually directed more to an institution and its goals than to a particular person. People with the gift often have a wide range of abilities and talents that they can offer when needs arise. They can be counted on for almost any kind of help. It is another quiet gift, one that does not usually make headlines.

The three gifts in this cluster—mercy, helps and service—are essential for the complete health of the Body. I think they are found in almost every local church and in relatively high numbers compared to some of the other gifts. I believe the Bible makes special mention of them in 1 Corinthians 12:22 when it says, "Much more those members of the body, which seem to be more feeble, are necessary."

The Gifts of Prophecy, Tongues and Interpretation

These three gifts, prophecy, tongues and interpretation, fall naturally together in a cluster because they, more than other gifts (except possibly the gifts of faith and discernment of spirits), are what might be called "revelatory." By this I mean that new information from God is transmitted directly to human beings via the person with the gift. Revelation of a kind actually occurs. This is not to be confused with the revelation of God that is contained in Scripture. We believe that Scripture is inerrant in all it affirms and that God did a special thing in inspiring the authors of Scripture to preserve the unique place of the Bible among all of the world's writings. It is the written Word of God and there is no other.

The gifts we are discussing here are not *the* Word *of* God, they are *a* word *from* God. The people who transmit God's word through spiritual gifts are not inerrant. Revelation that comes through prophecy or tongues is always subject to examination in the light of the written Word of God. The first test of whether a prophecy is true has to be its conformity to the Scriptures. For example, I vaguely recall that years ago a man drove his car at 80 miles per hour through the busy streets of an Ohio city and killed three people. When interviewed later he said he did it because God told him to. We know that this was a false prophecy because it cannot be reconciled with the ethical teachings of the Bible.

Those Christians who have the gift of discernment of spirits are readily able to tell the difference between true prophecy and false prophecy. They should be encouraged in the exercise of that gift. For the rest of us it is more difficult, but not impossible.

A mistake enthusiastic believers sometimes make who discover that some in their midst have the gifts of prophecy and/or tongues, is to pull back on studying, teaching, and preaching the Bible. They feel that these gifts which are more direct and require less effort than lengthy Bible study, are all they need. The gifts might be true gifts, but the believers who have them horribly misuse them. Anything that dilutes the supreme and unquestioned authority of the Scriptures must be resisted as a ploy of the devil.

On the other extreme there are some people who try to deny that God speaks today through prophecy and tongues because they are so fervent in their desire to preserve the uniqueness and authority of Scripture. Their motive is commendable, but they need to understand that this is not an either-or decision, it is both-and. The combination of biblical teaching about the gifts and the experience of innumerable sane Christian brothers and sisters forces us to the conclusion that God does speak today in a direct and specific way to particular needs and situations as He did among the ancient people of Israel and among Christians in the first century. His chief (but not exclusive) vehicles for doing this are the gifts of prophecy, tongues and interpretation.

Gift 1: The Gift of Prophecy

The gift of prophecy is the special ability that God gives to certain members of the Body of Christ to receive and communicate an immediate message of God to His people through a divinely-anointed utterance.

Since the word "prophecy" today usually means predicting the future, it is difficult for some people to realize that the biblical use of the word includes not only the future but also a word for the present. In fact the gift of prophecy has been used much more for dealing with present situations than with future events. The meaning of the Greek word is basically "to speak forth" or "to speak for another." Those who have the gift of prophecy receive personal inspiration as to God's purpose in a concrete situation. God speaks through the prophet.

The prophet can err. Therefore he or she must be open to correction by the rest of the Body. True prophets are willing for this. They want their words to be tested, and when they are wrong they will admit it. They want their prophecies to be confirmed by the Word of God and by the Body as a whole.

Those who receive the benefit of the gift of prophecy can expect comfort, guidance, warning, encouragement, admonition, judgment and edification. Some prophecies are directed by God to individuals, some to the Body of Christ as a whole. In any case they should be received as authentic and authoritative messages. As Michael Green says, "The Spirit has taken over and addresses the hearers directly through [the prophet]. That is the essence of prophecy."[2] Once the spiritual gift is confirmed by the Body, the person with the gift should be highly respected, and his or her words received with confidence.

Some authors equate the gift of prophecy with good preaching. They tend to question the assertion that God is pleased to speak today through those who profess to have the gift and who are channels for God to speak a definite specific message. I personally do not adhere to this viewpoint, but at the same time it is widely held by distinguished Christian leaders and even written into the official policies of local churches and denominations. Because I respect these people so much I have to keep an open mind. After all, I may well be the one who is wrong. But having said this, let me add that I have not yet found a correlation between one or the other and church growth. God seems to bless His children who take either view, providing other church-growth principles are in operation. My counsel is to trust God to show you which viewpoint you and your group should hold, and believe that God will work through your segment of the Body for His glory and for the salvation of souls. He won't disappoint you.

One of the varieties of the gift of prophecy is related to social consciousness. As can be observed by studying the prophets of the Old Testament especially, social concern was very prominent. People with this variety of the gift today tend to be politically-minded. They are sensitive to social trends nationally and internationally. They like to use their energies in making pronouncements concerning public righteousness and they are usually severely critical of contemporary culture. This gift seemed to be dormant among evangelicals for some time, but within the past 15 years it has been discovered and is being used by many to the great benefit of others of us who do not have the gift.

People with this socially-oriented variety of the gift of prophet are quite often freewheeling. Since their message is frequently unpopular, they would feel restrained if they were too closely tied to an institution. And many church institutions feel uncomfortable with such prophets around too much. Rarely, if ever, will a person with that kind of the gift of prophecy be the pastor of a growing church. They typically are suspicious of church growth. They will hardly ever have gifts of administration or leadership so they do not usually hold office. Besides, they tend to shun church bureaucracies and prefer to be outside critics.

Prophecy and Knowledge

A minor area of disagreement that I find with some authors in the classical Pentecostal tradition concerns the relationship between the gift of knowledge and the gift of prophecy. They would not agree with the definition of the gift of knowledge that I proposed earlier in this chapter. They tend to define the gift of the "word of knowledge" in much the same way I have defined the gift of prophecy. I have studied this point of view fairly carefully. One thing I notice is that such authors have a very difficult time distinguishing between the gift of knowledge, the gift of wisdom and the gift of prophecy. The three appear to be almost synonymous in their writings.[3]

A fine book, *Hear His Voice*, has been written by Douglas Wead on the word of knowledge. As I read it, I came to the conclusion that he was really writing on the gift of prophecy under another name. I was gratified when I came to a passage where he admits that "some will maintain that it should be categorized as a part of the gift of prophecy."[4] I for one do. But I agree with his following statement that, no matter what name we give it, "this ability to receive information through extrasensory means was a gift which operated in the New Testament Church as a gift of the Holy Spirit."[5]

I was relieved to see that not all classical Pentecostals hold this view of the gift of knowledge. Donald Gee, for example, tends to agree with me that the gift of knowledge relates more to teaching than it does to prophecy, and he has a long section in which he argues his point.[6] In doing so, he at the same time says, "I wish especially to make clear that I have welcomed interpretations that differ from my own regarding the word of wisdom and the word of knowledge." So do I, mainly because I believe that the label one gives to the phenomenon makes little difference in the long run for the growth of the church.

But I also feel personally that I need to explain my position, particularly since when we are dealing with the gift of knowledge we are dealing with one of the gifts I perceive to have in my own gift-mix.

Some who are not familiar with the gift of prophecy

firsthand might be wishing at this point for an example as to how it works. Many of the books on spiritual gifts written from the charismatic point of view give numerous examples. In this regard I recommend a whole book written just on the gift of prophecy by a Catholic author, Bruce Yocum, called *Prophecy*.[7] The book by Douglas Wead I just referred to is also packed with illustrations of prophecy (although he attributes them to the word of knowledge). To conclude, let me select one of Wead's anecdotes involving the well-known master of ceremonies on the "700 Club," Pat Robertson.

During a telecast, as Robertson tells the story, "As we were praying God showed me that there was a person whose right forearm had been broken and was in a cast. God was healing it. As I was leaving the studio at the end of the program, I was approached by two women in their middle years. The older of the two had her forearm in a cast. When I saw her, I was asked to pray for them. I replied, 'The work has already been done.' "[8]

Sure enough. The lady returned to her doctor who x-rayed the arm and found that the bone, which had been crushed, was mended with almost two inches of new bone tissue. The arm had healed and he removed the cast. This is a fairly frequent occurrence for Robertson who apparently has the gift.

Gift 14: The Gift of Tongues

In my studies of the literature on spiritual gifts, I have read so much about the gift of tongues that I have become saturated. I believe that tongues has received a disproportionate amount of press in the past few years. Of course much of this has to do with the debate as to whether tongues is the "initial physical sign" of the baptism of believers in the Holy Ghost, as the constitution of the Assemblies of God, for example, affirms.

Even recognized charismatics do not agree with one another on this. I am not going to discuss this issue because (a) I could not possibly add any light to what has already been written and (b) I can discern no connection between this debate and church growth.

The gift of tongues is the special ability that God gives to certain members of the Body of Christ (A) to speak to God in a language they have never learned and/or (B) to receive and communicate an immediate message of God to His people through a divinely-anointed utterance in a language they have never learned.

This is the only one of the 27 gifts that I feel must be broken down into an A part and a B part. The first variety of the gift of tongues might be called "private tongues" and the second variety "public tongues."

Private tongues are often referred to as "prayer language." No accompanying gift of interpretation is involved. The biblical text most descriptive of this is 1 Corinthians 14:28 where Paul says that tongues without interpretation should not be used in the church, but rather the person who has such a gift should "speak to himself, and to God." Since this is highly experiential, I am going to describe it by using the experiences of a Christian brother.

Robert Tuttle is an esteemed colleague of mine on the faculty of Fuller Seminary and a United Methodist minister. His gift is private tongues. He says, "There are times in my devotional life when I can no longer find words to express my 'innards.' . . . At that point I allow the Holy Spirit to pray through me in a language that I did not learn. Believe me, I know what it means to learn a language. I struggle with the biblical languages every day . . . I say a language because I believe it to be a language. My vocabulary is growing. I know enough about language to be able to identify sentence structure.

My unknown tongue or prayer language has periods, commas, and exclamation points. It is a marvelous gift."[9]

Not all students of spiritual gifts agree that this is a real language. Some professional linguists have tape-recorded persons speaking in tongues and said they find no linguistic structure. But since they haven't taped all tongues, maybe the ones they did tape were so-called ecstatic utterances while others, like Tuttle's, may be languages. In any case, I find the point to be academic because whether ecstatic utterances or structured languages, the function is the same. This function has been described by Harald Bredesen, pastor of North County Christian Center in San Marcos, California, in several postulates:

1. "Tongues enables our spirits to communicate directly with God above and beyond the power of our minds to understand."
2. "Tongues liberates the Spirit of God within us."
3. "Tongues enable the spirit to take its place of ascendancy over soul and body."
4. "Tongues is God's provision for catharsis, therefore important to our mental health."
5. "Tongues meets our needs for a whole new language for worship, prayer and praise."[10]

These statements do not need comment. There is no question that they reflect the self-perception of one who has and uses the gift of tongues.

I suppose that this gift of private tongues is the most commonly projected of all the spiritual gifts. People who have it find it so simple and so natural that they are inclined to say that anybody can do it. They quote Paul's statement, "I would that ye all spoke with tongues" (1 Cor. 14:5), but perhaps make it mean much more than Paul intended in the context of the abuse of tongues in

Corinth. If there is any such thing as a role of tongues, I suppose it would fit here, but perhaps this is one gift that has no corresponding role. I see the need for a great deal more study here before anyone can be dogmatic. Meanwhile, I do know personally some wonderfully mature Christian brothers and sisters who have sincerely tried, for an extended period of time, to pray in tongues with no success. To say that they have not been filled with the Spirit would, in their cases, be both inaccurate and unfair. It is best to say that they simply do not have the gift of tongues.

Gift 15: The Gift of Interpretation

Part B or public tongues is intimately related to the gift of interpretation. Without interpretation the gift is useless and has no part in the church (see 1 Cor. 14:27, 28).

The gift of interpretation is the special ability that God gives to certain members of the Body of Christ to make known in the vernacular the message of one who speaks in tongues.

Quite often, but not always, tongues-interpretation functions as a hyphenated gift. Michael Green says, "Though some men have the gift of interpretation who cannot themselves speak in tongues, this is unusual; for the most part it is those who already have tongues who gain this further gift of interpretation."[11] This means that some people give messages in public in tongues and immediately interpret what they themselves have said. In other cases one will give the message and another will interpret.

Not much needs to be said about public tongues except that it is a function equivalent to prophecy. The whole argument of 1 Corinthians 14 develops this equivalence. What we previously said about the gift of prophecy, then, applies equally to public tongues.

Just by way of example I will relate a secondhand anecdote that I received from a very reliable source. It involves a group of believers in a remote Guatemalan village. A severe drought had devastated the area and the village was on the verge of extinction. The Christians prayed and God spoke to the group through a message in tongues. He told them to go up on a hill which was owned by the Christians and dig a well. It seemed to be one of the most illogical places to do it, but they obeyed, even in the face of the ridicule of the unbelievers in the village. The ridicule changed to astonishment, however, when they soon struck an abundant supply of water and the entire village was saved. Many unbelievers also were saved when they saw the power of God. Maybe this is what Paul had in mind when he wrote, "Tongues are for a sign, not to them that believe, but to them that believe not" (1 Cor. 14:22).

One rather parenthetical observation needs to be made before moving on to another cluster of gifts. Some people have gone as missionaries to other linguistic groups and have begun speaking the second language without ever having learned it. Documentation of this is at least abundant enough to satisfy me, even though I have not seen it firsthand. Is this the gift of tongues? In my opinion, no. I regard it simply as a miracle that God performed on that certain occasion. And I am encouraged to find that one of the key classical Pentecostal authors, Donald Gee, agrees with me concerning this point.[12]

The Gifts of Miracles and Healing

Whereas prophecy and tongues are immediate *words* of supernatural origin, miracles and healing are immediate *deeds* of supernatural origin. In both cases human beings with spiritual gifts are the channels through which God does a remarkable work.

Gift 12: The Gift of Miracles

The gift of miracles is the special ability that God gives to certain members of the Body of Christ to serve as human intermediaries through whom it pleases God to perform powerful acts that are perceived by observers to have altered the ordinary course of nature.

Notice that this definition does not close the door to the performance of miracles that may later be "disproved" by the application of Western scientific methodologies. I have read lengthy explanations, for example, of why people who were raised from the dead in Indonesia were not really raised from the dead. Some Western investigators apparently went to Indonesia and concluded that, according to their Western definitions of death, it did not happen.

This would be amusing if it were not so pathetic. God performed the miracles for Indonesians, not for Americans or Europeans. If Indonesians really and truly thought, in terms of their own worldview, that the dead had been raised, the miracle happened. The ordinary course of nature had been altered. If through observing this, Indonesian believers were strengthened in their faith and Indonesian unbelievers were convinced of the power of God and became followers of Jesus Christ, the purpose of the miracle was accomplished. Even within our Western worldview the most advanced scientists and doctors of jurisprudence have not been able to agree precisely on when death actually occurs. Why, then, superimpose our inexact worldview on the Indonesians' inexact worldview? It proves very little.

Because of our subtle commitment to naturalism, we Westerners tend to be suspect of anything clearly supernatural. That is undoubtedly one reason why we do not see many miracles working in our churches here today. But it is no reason to look with sophisticated skepticism upon the working of God's miracles in other cultures which are much more open to supernaturalism than our own.

And my perception is that our own culture is gradually becoming more open to supernaturalism. The increasing popularity of the transcendent, the rise of Oriental religions and the occult, the phenomenal expansion of the charismatic movement itself—all are indicators that many Americans may be fed up with the unsatisfying naturalism that modern science and technology have attempted to make part and parcel of our culture. If so, the way may be open as never before for the gift of miracles to become evident in our American churches.

Some will fear such a manifestation of God's power because the gift so easily can be abused. This is true, but not an adequate reason for hastily rejecting the gift of miracles, it seems to me. Yes, God will and does bless churches that do not permit miracles. But to justify an aversion to miracles from a biblical point of view is not easy. The aversion is probably much more cultural than biblical. I agree with Kenneth Gangel when he says, "We dare not be guided in our understanding of spiritual gifts by a fear born of unhappy experiences nor an exegesis which results from hermeneutical myopia."[13]

Gift 11: The Gift of Healing

The gift of healing is the special ability that God gives to certain members of the Body of Christ to serve as human intermediaries through whom it pleases God to cure illness and restore health apart from the use of natural means.

In one sense the gift of healing can be understood as

a specialized manifestation of the gift of miracles, but the two are mentioned separately in the Bible, so we separate them also. Obviously, healing has to do with human illness specifically, although it includes all kinds of human illnesses. The biblical reference to the gift in 1 Corinthians 12:28 is literally gifts (plural) of healings (plural). This seems to imply that there are many varieties of the gift for different kinds of illnesses.

To restrict the gift of healing just to physical diseases is not proper. The gift can also be used to cure mental, emotional and spiritual illnesses. Agnes Sanford, a contemporary with the gift of healing, has the gift of "healing the memory." Another, Ruth Carter Stapleton, deals with "inner healing." There may be many more varieties.

The gift of healing does not give a person supernatural power over disease. He or she is simply a channel through whom God works when He desires to heal. People with the gift of healing have no power to empty the hospitals unless God decides to do that through them. No one fully understands God's position on sickness and health. Sometimes, as we know from Job, sickness is part of the total plan of God and He permits it. The apostle Paul had a "thorn in the flesh" which in all probability was a physical problem of some kind, but God chose not to remove it (see 2 Cor. 12:7-9). And, furthermore, healing is not permanent. As far as we know, all the people whom Jesus Himself healed eventually died.

The gift of healing does not make doctors and nurses obsolete. In many cases God is pleased to use modern medical means of healing, although this should not be confused with the gift of healing. Christian doctors by and large are using natural talents, not a spiritual gift. Part of the definition of the gift is "apart from the use of natural means." When Timothy had a stomach ailment, Paul did not send him a handkerchief that he had touched so that Timothy could be healed through it. Paul had used the handkerchiefs in Ephesus to good effect (see Acts 19:12), but he recommended wine to Timothy in this case (see 1 Tim. 5:23). Sometimes natural means are in order, sometimes God chooses to heal miraculously. The person with the gift cannot manipulate God. He or she is simply a frequently-used channel.

God has healed me personally in both ways. Most of my sicknesses have been cured by doctors or known remedies. One time, however, He cured me directly. Some years ago in Bolivia I had an open sore on my neck that had been operated on and would not heal, so I was scheduled for further surgery. Then E. Stanley Jones came to town and some of us missionaries went to hear him. His meeting turned out to be a healing service. During the service I knew I had been healed. When I got home I took the bandage off and it was still full of puss. But I thanked the Lord, went to bed, and the next morning it was perfectly well. The doctor was astounded, but he was a Christian and we praised the Lord together!

As I researched the Pentecostal movement in Latin America and analyzed its amazing growth over the past 25 years, I found that one of the key factors contributing to its growth is faith healing. Latin American Pentecostals tend to believe that God can and will heal apart from natural means, and He does it frequently in their midst. Non-Pentecostals tend to believe that God can heal but not that He will, so He doesn't seem to do it very much at all.[14] If the faith is not there, the healing does not happen as Jesus' disciples learned. They were "of little faith," and so are many of us today.

I have a strong hunch that more of an emphasis on divine healing would help churches grow here in America. Most Americans are thankful for the advanced state of medical science and the almost universal accessibility of physicians. However, I believe that God would also love to do some healing Himself if we only permitted Him to do it. I am with Robert Tuttle who says, "I long for the day when the church will expect physical and emotional healing just as readily as it would conversion or the new birth."[15]

In fact, one church in Philadelphia, St. Stephen's Episcopal Church, began a regular healing ministry in 1942, and it helped the church to grow. The leader of this was Alfred Price who has developed the idea of "sacramental healing" both theologically and experientially. I do not know if Alfred Price has the gift of healing, but I have been in a church where the sacrament of healing was practiced only as a Christian role, not with the specific gift of healing. This is the Wesley Methodist Church of Hamilton, Bermuda. There Pastor Ross Bailey holds a healing service the third Sunday night of every month. He simply believes that healing should be part of the total ministry of the church as naturally as Bible study groups or serving the Lord's Supper. It is not an emotional meeting at all. Rather there is a printed liturgy the congregation goes through. But God acts and people are wonderfully healed in many ways.[16]

All too few churches do this. As individuals, whether or not we have the gift of healing, we should be ready to pray for the sick and anoint them with oil (see Jas. 5:14,15). It seems to me that churches that do not make this a regular part of their philosophy of ministry (and this would include the vast majority of American churches) might be missing out on a very powerful dynamic of church growth. How I would love to see hundreds of American churches release this power of God in their midst and through it draw thousands of men and women to Jesus Christ and His love.

Notes

1. Ralph W. Neighbour, Jr., *This Gift Is Mine* (Nashville: Broadman Press, 1974), p. 72.
2. Michael Green, *I Believe in the Holy Spirit* (Grand Rapids: Wm. B. Eerdmans Publishing Co., 1975), p. 172.
3. See, for example, Harold Horton, *The Gifts of the Spirit* (Springfield: Gospel Publishing House, 1975), chapters 4 and 5; and Jim McNair, *Love and Gifts* (Minneapolis: Bethany Fellowship, 1976), p. 26.
4. R. Douglas Wead, *Hear His Voice* (Carol Stream, IL: Creation House, 1976), p. 100.
5. *Ibid.*
6. Donald Gee, *Concerning Spiritual Gifts* (Springfield: Gospel Publishing House, 1972), pp. 111-119.
7. Bruce Yocum, *Prophecy* (Ann Arbor, MI: Word of Life, 1976).
8. Wead, *Hear His Voice*, p. 120.
9. Robert G. Tuttle, *The Partakers* (Nashville: Abingdon Press, 1974), p. 82.
10. Harald Bredesen, "The Gift of Tongues," *Logos Journal* (March, 1978), pp. 19-24.
11. Green, *I Believe in the Holy Spirit*, p. 167.
12. Gee, *Concerning Spiritual Gifts*, p. 97.
13. Kenneth O. Gangel, *You and Your Spiritual Gift* (Chicago: Moody Press, 1975), p. 59.
14. This is expanded in C. Peter Wagner, *What Are We Missing?* (Carol Stream, IL: Creation House, 1978), chapter 9.
15. Tuttle, *The Partakers*, p. 70.
16. Those wishing more information on this kind of healing ministry should write to The International Order of St. Luke the Physician, 1161 E. Jersey Street, Elizabeth, NJ 07201.

9.
Five Steps Toward Growing Through Gifts

All the good theories in the world about spiritual gifts will not be worth more than a pleasant head trip if their dynamics are not released for effective operation in local congregations. The purpose of this final chapter is to propose some guidelines as to how this can happen.

After only a short time of conversation it is fairly easy to know whether a given person comes from a church that is aware of spiritual gifts and encouraging their use. Many Christians are either ignorant of spiritual gifts beyond a very superficial awareness or they are surprisingly bashful about making reference to their own spiritual gift or gifts. Some are unsure. Some feel they would be boasting if they mentioned their gift. Some don't want to be held accountable for its use, so they keep it to themselves.

I was recently in a meeting of a small group of Christian leaders from around the world. Most of them were considered part of the elite of their country, and their names would be recognized as Christian household words. In a session of sharing (which I did not lead, by the way) each one around the circle was asked to praise God for a specific spiritual gift. I quickly took a pencil out to jot down what the responses would be, and here they are:

"Preaching the gospel"
"The Holy Spirit"
"Jesus Christ"
"The life-giving Spirit"
"Billy Graham"
"Loved ones and children"
"Teaching"
"Brothers and sisters in Christ"

I will admit that I was the one who mentioned "teaching" as my idea of what a spiritual gift really is. I surmise that "preaching the gospel" was meant to refer to the gift of evangelist. But I was disappointed that of a group like this only 25 percent could intelligently articulate a spiritual gift. If it were back 15 or 20 years ago I might understand it. But if these are leaders, what must the percentage be among grassroots Christians? As in Corinth there is still ignorance of spiritual gifts (see 1 Cor. 12:1).

The time is ripe for Christians all over America, in every church, to begin to think soberly of themselves (see Rom. 12:3). They cannot do this, of course, with any air of pride. But neither should they do it by putting up a facade of false humility that blinds them and others around them to the function that God has given them in the Body of Christ.

I am going to outline five steps that are designed to

help get your church off dead center and put in operation the wonderful power that God has already provided in the gifts He has given. The five steps, just as this whole book, are addressed to both clergy and laity. But I need to stress right here two assumptions I am making preliminary to the five steps. I am assuming first of all that the pastor of your church is convinced that discovering, developing and using spiritual gifts is the will of God for his congregation and that he is willing to take an active leadership role in the process. I am also assuming that your pastor wants your church to grow and believes it is the will of God.

The two assumptions are based on everything I tried to say in chapter 5, the chapter on the pastor. The pastor is God's key person for the growth of a local church, and if for some reason or other he is either indifferent or opposed to church growth or spiritual gifts, my advice is to postpone these five steps or they will abort. I frankly hope that this book itself will help change the mind of many a reluctant pastor, but if it or other books or seminars or personal exhortation do not do the trick, continue to pray and wait for God's better timing.

Step 1: Agree on a Philosophy of Ministry

The benefits of each local church having a well-articulated philosophy of ministry have been mentioned several times already.[1] Part of the philosophy of ministry ought to be a clear statement on what the church believes and expects in the way of spiritual gifts. If your church has a stated philosophy of ministry and it does not include a section on spiritual gifts, I suggest it be amended.

Any program you launch for discovering and using spiritual gifts will be molded by your philosophy of ministry. You need to decide such things as:

1. Which spiritual gifts do we expect God to give to our church in our particular gift-mix? Are we open to all 27, or how many might there be? Will we look for 19 or 9 or how many?
2. Are we open to the sign gifts such as tongues and prophecy and healings? If yes, should they be used in public or only in private? If public, should they be used in all services or only in certain ones?
3. Do we believe that baptism in the Holy Spirit is a second work of grace or do all Christians receive it when they are saved? If a second work of grace, do we believe that speaking in tongues is the initial physical sign that tells us it has happened?
4. What position do we take in regard to new people who come into our church but who disagree with our views on spiritual gifts? Or with current members who change their views? Are we cordial to this, do we just tolerate it, or do we recommend that such persons seek fellowship in a more compatible church?

My recommendation is that as the leaders of the church sit down to discuss these issues they do not become overly self-conscious. Above all, do not make a decision just because X-church down the street does it that way. Look at it with the same spirit that we Christians have learned to look at baptism. Some churches baptize infants by sprinkling. Some churches will neither baptize infants nor baptize by sprinkling. Some churches which immerse dip the person three times instead of only once. Some dip them three times forward and some dip them three times backward. Quakers don't believe in water baptism at all. My own church, a Congregational Church, doesn't think any of this is essential so we baptize both infants and adults by either sprinkling or immersion, and I suppose if someone requested it we would baptize them three times forward. If some don't want to be baptized at all, we also accept them and love them on the same basis as the others.

Churches across America tend to accept the fact that God leads different churches to establish different philosophies of baptism, and none of us tends to feel self-conscious because we happen to hold a certain position. Let's follow this same pattern on spiritual gifts. Let's decide on our own philosophy of spiritual gifts, let's discover what particular gift-mix God has given our church, and let's praise God for other churches that have different philosophies of ministry.

If we do this, there will be two immediate benefits. First, Christian brotherhood will be enhanced. It is a tragedy that some local churches have split over spiritual gifts. The chances of this happening are almost nil when a clear philosophy of ministry is agreed upon. Not only will brothers and sisters in a local church love one another but feelings of envy, jealousy, competition or witch-hunting between churches will be reduced. Why not accept each others' differences and love each other in the Lord? I like the title of Peter Gillquist's book, *Let's Quit Fighting About the Holy Spirit.*[2]

The second benefit will be church growth. The more variety of churches and philosophies of ministry, the more people will be won to Christ. People themselves come in so many different varieties that many different kinds of churches are needed to win them to Christ. It would be a setback to effective evangelism if all churches somehow became the same. This is why in most cases church mergers ultimately end up with fewer members than the separate churches had before they merged.

Step 2: Initiate a Growth Process

Discovering, developing and using spiritual gifts can

be an end in itself, and it is a good end. In some cases this alone will help a church grow. But church growth is complex and the dynamic of spiritual gifts is only one of many church-growth principles. Therefore in most cases a program of putting spiritual gifts to use will not be sufficient for maximizing the growth potential of a church. When gifts are discovered they have to have channels through which to be used effectively.

Few things can be more frustrating than discovering a spiritual gift and not being able to use it in the church. In fact, pastors need to be aware that the church can lose members if this happens. They will simply transfer to some church where they are more useful.

It is impossible for me to explain in any detail here how to develop a growth process in the church. The most effective route I know of is for the pastor himself to take professional training in church growth, preferably on the Doctor of Ministry level.[3] The church should be willing to finance this for their own benefit as well as for the pastor's. Another highly valuable tool is the *Diagnostic Clinic* that has been developed by Fuller Evangelistic Association. This helps the pastor prepare for and lead a three-and-one-half-hour clinic with his church leaders that will give them an accurate picture of their growth potential.[4] An increasing number of professional church diagnosticians are also available to churches that feel a need for outside consultation and opinions.[5]

At the proper point in the growth process, the congregation as a whole needs to become excited and motivated for growth. No one has had more experience and success in doing this than the Institute for American Church Growth under the leadership of Win Arn. With seminars and films and games and posters and Sunday School curricula and books, they can build a new faith and expectation for church growth into most any congregation, provided the pastor wants it to happen.[6]

With whatever resources, denominational or interdenominational, beginning a sound growth process before starting to work on spiritual gifts will pay appreciable dividends.

Step 3: Structure for Gifts and Growth

I have recorded elsewhere my feelings on how a church needs to be structured administratively for growth.[7] One form of government that is popular in America, but that is usually counterproductive for growth in a large church is a congregational form of government. Most pastors of large, growing churches with traditionally congregational governments have somehow developed ways and means to streamline the structure. It is feasible for smaller churches, but when the membership begins to pass the 200 mark it becomes less and less effective.

The smoothest structure for growth is one which fully recognizes the leadership position of the pastor and frees him to utilize his spiritual gift or gifts. In many growing churches one board runs the church and the pastor is the chairman of the board and president of the corporation, or titles to that effect. When the church has a well thought-out philosophy of ministry this can operate well. The more boards and committees in a church the more chances for bickering, infighting and conflict of interests. They slow down the decision-making process sometimes almost to a standstill. In many churches there are far too many chiefs in proportion to Indians.

As I understand God's way of operating, there is one person and one person only who, under God, bears the chief responsibility for a local church—that person is the senior pastor. God will hold all members responsible for their church, of course, but none to the degree of the person who has accepted the top position of leadership. I believe that the attitude church members need to have toward their pastor is described in Hebrews 13:17: "Obey your leaders and follow their orders. They watch over your souls without resting, since they must give to God an account of their service. If you obey them, they will do their work gladly; if not, they will do it with sadness, and that would be of no help to you" (*TEV*).

Not enough sermons are preached on this text. It is extremely difficult for a pastor to preach a sermon on it in his own church because his motives can so easily be misinterpreted. That is why I continually bring it up and stress it. Since I am not a pastor I have few worries about being misinterpreted. But I do have a pastor over me and I try to apply it in my own attitude toward him and toward the staff. Many pastors are suffering untold personal grief and frustration because their people do not understand or practice the biblical principle of obedience to those in authority. The total effect of overlooking or neglecting this principle is that it becomes an obstruction to church growth.

Parkinson's Law and Church Growth

Research done by Kent Tucker indicates that in many churches 85 percent of available time is given to management while only 15 percent of time is given to ministry.[8] The basic growth problem here is the proportion of available time spent in administrative and organizational matters as compared to the time spent in actual ministry. This is horribly inefficient. No corporation could last a month with such a structure. Parkinson's Law, which says that work increases to fill the time available for doing it, is rampant in most churches. Committees and boards can be incredibly busy, but in the end get very little done in terms of the ministry objectives of the church.

The First Baptist Church of Modesto discovered this problem in 1967 and has been growing faster ever since. That is when their present pastor, Bill Yaeger, arrived and streamlined the church administration for growth. Previously the church showed a decadal decline of 0.8 percent. Over a period of 10 years only three new converts were baptized. Under Yaeger's leadership the church reorganized its structure by going from a multiple-board church to a one-board church. Yaeger says, "When we have this simplified organizational structure, people are then free to be involved in evangelism and discipleship."[9] They calculate that at present 97.1 percent of the time lay-people give to the church goes into ministry, and only 2.9 percent goes toward managing the affairs of the church. The growth rate of First Baptist over the 10 years following the change has been 388 percent! At least one church has not allowed Parkinson's Law to halt its growth.

Once people are freed from organizational duties for which most are not gifted, they can use their gifts in jobs that they are more suited for. It comes as a surprise to many church leaders to find out just how their personnel is deployed when they study it carefully.

A helpful typology that is widely used in church growth today is the "five classes of workers" scheme that was first presented by Donald McGavran, the founder of the church-growth movement.[10] To recap briefly, they are:

Class I workers: unpaid workers whose responsibility is to work within the congregation. They include Sunday School teachers, ushers, trustees, deacons, choir members, and many more.

Class II workers: unpaid workers whose responsibility

takes them outside the church to those who are unbelievers. They include those who do evangelism or minister with gifts of mercy or service.

Class III workers: unpaid or partially paid workers who take responsibility for establishing new congregations or missions.

Class IV workers: paid staff members of the church.

Class V workers: denominational executives or church bureaucrats of one kind or another whose responsibility covers many churches.

The most crucial area for mobilizing a church for growth is the proportion of Class I workers to Class II workers. Without going into detail here, I might just mention that the recommended goal is 40 percent of church members as Class I workers and 20 percent as Class II workers. How to calculate this has been described in detail in a manual called *Worker Analysis* published by Fuller Evangelistic Association.[11] This is a helpful tool to begin to work out a growth structure for your church. Once it is done, you are ready to concentrate more specifically on the spiritual gifts.

Step 4: Unwrap the Spiritual Gifts

Think of your church experience as a Christmas day. The tree is up and the gifts are there. All the family has to do is unwrap them. Your church is ready to grow. God has provided the gifts, but few people know what they are. Now is the time to unwrap them!

As I see it, there are six different items on the checklist for moving into a process of getting a strong dynamic of spiritual gifts going in your church.

A. Motivate the congregation from the pulpit. Since the pastor is the one who needs to lead the church into growth, his ideas need to be heard from the pulpit. One pastor I know of preached 22 consecutive sermons on spiritual gifts with dramatic results both in terms of people finding their own gifts and in explosive church growth. Many other pastors have found that a series of sermons on spiritual gifts has made a visible difference in growth. Pastors of churches that become structured around spiritual gifts not only preach such series but they continually mention spiritual gifts in their other sermons. And they do not assume that just one series of sermons is enough. Year after year they preach on the subject from different points of view to inform new members and to reinforce older members.

When the pastor talks a lot about spiritual gifts it makes it easier for the people to talk about them. They realize that it is an "in" thing, and the tone created by a strong pulpit ministry on gifts can be helpful in all areas of church life.

B. Study the biblical teaching on gifts. Not only should the people hear about spiritual gifts from the pulpit, but they also should study about gifts themselves. This can be done in small groups, in special study sessions, in Sunday School classes or alone at home. David C. Cook has a fine Sunday School curriculum component called *Congratulations! You're Gifted.*[12] The West Indies Mission publishes a helpful self-study manual on gifts called *Spiritual Gifts*, written by Bobby Clinton.[13] Fuller Evangelistic Association also has an excellent Bible study which is designed either for individual or group study.[14] Many denominations have in-house material on spiritual gifts. The Church of the Nazarene, for example, has developed a pack of materials specifically aimed at Wesleyan or holiness denominations.[15]

Bible study will help the congregation become familiar with what the gifts are, how they fit into the Body of Christ, and what they might mean personally to each person.

C. Help adults discover their gifts. I have used the word "adults" advisedly here, because not every Christian of every age is ready for coming to terms with his or her spiritual gift. My rule of thumb is that if you're 18 and do not know your spiritual gifts, don't worry; you're probably too young. However, if you're 25 and still don't know your spiritual gift, it is time to start worrying. The ability to discover spiritual gifts, in my understanding, is a function of emotional maturity. Emotionally mature people are ready to know their gifts, but emotional maturity comes at different ages for different people. Some are emotionally mature at 20, others are not yet emotionally mature at 30.

New Christians who are emotionally mature should be expected to discover their gifts within 4 to 12 months, depending on a variety of factors. One of the first things they should learn is that God has given them a spiritual gift and that it is waiting for them to discover.

Young people need to be aware of spiritual gifts as early as possible. I have seen an excellent first-grade curriculum produced by the Lutheran Church Missouri Synod for their parochial schools that teaches children from the beginning that they are part of a larger Body and that their contribution to the Body is very important to God. High school and college age young people do well to experiment with whatever gifts possible, but they should keep open minds as far as coming to any definite conclusions are concerned. I have observed many seminary students who know the biblical teaching on spiritual gifts but who have not yet discovered theirs with any kind of certainty.

D. Hold a spiritual gifts workshop. One of the frustrations I felt during about 20 years of teaching spiritual gifts was that when I got through and people understood the theory, I had nowhere to take them from there. Most people who learn about spiritual gifts want to know what theirs is, but I couldn't help them much.

That is why I was so delighted when, about a year ago, the Church Growth Department of Fuller Evangelistic Association came up with a first-rate workshop on spiritual gifts that can be used in any church group. The leader's guide has two cassette tapes of my lecture on the subject, some art work for overhead projections, and a student workbook with the answers. During the workshop, which takes about six hours, each student fills in his or her own workbook which contains, among other things, a Modified Houts Questionnaire. This is a list of 125 questions which go a long way in helping each person begin to get a handle on the gift or gifts that God has given them. Then they get together in small groups of five or six people, who know one another, to talk over the results of the questionnaires and see if they can help one another begin to discover gifts. It has been tested in scores of churches with very encouraging results.[16]

This is not the only discovery tool available. Several churches have developed their own. The Western Baptist Seminary, for example, has produced a "Spiritual Gift Inventory" by Gordon McMinn. It deals with 12 gifts and is scored on a computer.[17] The Southern Baptists have a table game for discovering gifts called "Nexus."[18] Undoubtedly the resources for gift discovery will increase both in variety and in sophistication.

E. Set a schedule for accountability. Some churches make the mistake of holding a spiritual gifts workshop as if it were just another pleasant and inspiring spiritual exercise. Then they go home and begin something else. No definite plans are made to follow through, so the net result in some cases is negligible as far as church growth is concerned.

As the spiritual gift process gets under way, be sure

to set goals for the discovery of spiritual gifts. One good goal might be that 50 percent of the adults will be able to describe their own spiritual gift or gifts in 12 months and that 20 percent more will be in the process. Each group needs to develop some system to see that it happens. People need to be held accountable to each other for discovering their gifts and then for using them.

F. Continue the experience indefinitely. Discovering, developing and using spiritual gifts should be no more an on-again-off-again part of church life than prayer or Bible study or holy Communion. The experience should become a permanent part of the life-style of the congregation. It needs to be stimulated with books and sermons and Sunday School lessons, and task-oriented groups that help people put their gifts to use. Timothy let his gift fall into disuse and Paul had to prod him (see 1 Tim. 4:14). It will happen to us also if we are not on guard against it.

Perhaps the recent action of St. Paul Lutheran Church in Detroit, Michigan could be an example for others interested in building spiritual gifts into their growth process. The church, now growing at 270 percent per decade, has found spiritual gifts to be a vital key. As a result, Pastor Wayne Pohl has added a new full-time staff member Arthur Beyer, with the title "Minister of Spiritual Gifts."

Step 5: Expect God's Blessing

Teaching on spiritual gifts was not invented by some management efficiency consultant or by some department of church growth or by some theological seminary or even by some church council. The teaching on spiritual gifts comes directly from the Word of God. That gives us the assurance we need to say with confidence that it is God's way for His people to operate with one another. It is the way to do God's work whether caring for each other or learning more about the faith or celebrating the resurrection of Jesus Christ or reaching out to the lost with the message of God's love. It is the way to bring about the kind of church growth that builds the whole person and the whole Body of Christ.

Faith is the key. Without faith it is impossible to please God (see Heb. 11:6). Faith is expectation, expectation that God has something better for us. Expectation that we can be the people God wants us to be. Expectation that He has gifted us and that we will be richly fulfilled if we are doing His will through using spiritual gifts.

Faith tells us that God wants His church to grow. He wants His lost sheep found and brought into the fold. And He will do it through the gifts He has given to each of us for His glory.

Notes

1. Those desiring help in formulating a general philosophy of ministry for their church should write for the four-part *Pastor's Planning Workbook* available from Fuller Evangelistic Association, Box 989, Pasadena, California 91102. Part Two deals specifically with the philosophy of ministry.
2. Peter E. Gillquist, *Let's Quit Fighting About the Holy Spirit* (Grand Rapids: Zondervan Publishing House, 1974).
3. The only accredited Doctor of Ministry program I am aware of that has a concentration (up to 70 percent) in church growth is at Fuller Theological Seminary. For information on requirements both for credit and audit write to the Director of Continuing Education, Fuller Theological Seminary, 135 North Oakland Avenue, Pasadena, California 91101. Seminars in this program cover 12-day periods.
4. Information on the *Diagnostic Clinic* is available from Fuller Evangelistic Association, Box 989, Pasadena, California 91102.
5. Many denominations have church diagnosticians on their national and/or regional staffs. Among those who work interdenominationally I recommend Lyle Schaller, Yokefellow Institute, 530 N. Brainard, Naperville, Illinois 60540, and the staff of Fuller Evangelistic Association's Department of Church Growth, Box 989, Pasadena, California, 91102, under the direction of Carl George.
6. For further information write Institute for American Church Growth, 150 South Los Robles Avenue, Suite 600, Pasadena, California 91101.
7. See, for example, C. Peter Wagner, *Your Church Can Grow* (Glendale: Regal Books, 1976), pp. 61-66.

8. Kent A. Tucker, "A Church Growth Study of the First Baptist Church of Modesto" (Pasadena: Fuller Seminary, unpublished Doctor of Ministry paper, 1978), p. 37.
9. *Ibid.*, p. 38.
10. This was first published in Donald A. McGavran and Win C. Arn's *How to Grow a Church* (Glendale: Regal Books, 1973), pp. 89-97.
11. The *Worker Analysis* manual is part of the *Diagnostic Clinic* mentioned above, but is also available separately from Fuller Evangelistic Association, Box 989, Pasadena, California 91102.
12. If this is not available in your local Christian bookstore or Sunday School supply house, write David C. Cook Publishing Co., 850 N. Grove Ave., Elgin, Illinois 60120.
13. Order from West Indies Mission, Inc., Box 343038, Coral Gables, Florida 33134.
14. Available from Fuller Evangelistic Association, Box 989, Pasadena, California 91102.
15. Available from Nazarene Publishing House, 6401 The Paseo, Kansas City, Missouri 64131.
16. Both the leader's guide and student workbooks can be ordered from Fuller Evangelistic Association, Box 989, Pasadena, California 91102.
17. This "Spiritual Gifts Inventory" may be ordered from Western Baptist Seminary Bookstore, 5511 S.E. Hawthorne Boulevard., Portland, Oregon 97215.
18. For more information on "Nexus" write The Sunday School Board of the Southern Baptist Convention, 127 Ninth Avenue North, Nashville, Tennessee 37234.

Appendix: What Are the Gifts? —A Summary

These 27 spiritual gifts are here listed in the order in which they were presented in chapter 2.

1. *Prophecy*: The gift of prophecy is the special ability that God gives to certain members of the Body of Christ to receive and communicate an immediate message of God to His people through a divinely-anointed utterance.
2. *Service*: The gift of service is the special ability that God gives to certain members of the Body of Christ to identify the unmet needs involved in a task related to God's work, and to make use of available resources to meet those needs and help accomplish the desired goals.
3. *Teaching*: The gift of teaching is the specal ability that God gives to certain members of the Body of Christ to com-

municate information relevant to the health and ministry of the Body and its members in such a way that others will learn.

4. *Exhortation*: The gift of exhortation is the special ability that God gives to certain members of the Body of Christ to minister words of comfort, consolation, encouragement and counsel to other members of the Body in such a way that they feel helped and healed.
5. *Giving*: The gift of giving is the special ability that God gives to certain members of the Body of Christ to contribute their material resources to the work of the Lord with liberality and cheerfulness.
6. *Leadership*: The gift of leadership is the special ability that God gives to certain members of the Body of Christ to set goals in accordance with God's purpose for the future and to communicate these goals to others in such a way that they voluntarily and harmoniously work together to accomplish those goals for the glory of God.
7. *Mercy*: The gift of mercy is the special ability that God gives to certain members of the Body of Christ to feel genuine empathy and compassion for individuals, both Christian and non-Christian, who suffer distressing physical, mental or emotional problems, and to translate that compassion into cheerfully-done deeds that reflect Christ's love and alleviate the suffering.
8. *Wisdom*: The gift of wisdom is special ability that God gives to certain members of the Body of Christ to know the mind of the Holy Spirit in such a way as to receive insight into how given knowledge may best be applied to specific needs arising in the Body of Christ.
9. *Knowledge*: The gift of knowledge is the special ability that God gives to certain members of the Body of Christ to discover, accumulate, analyze and clarify information and ideas that are pertinent to the growth and well-being of the Body.

10. *Faith*: The gift of faith is the special ability that God gives to certain members of the Body of Christ to discern with extraordinary confidence the will and purposes of God for the future of His work.
11. *Healing*: The gift of healing is the special ability that God gives to certain members of the Body of Christ to serve as human intermediaries through whom it pleases God to cure illness and restore health apart from the use of natural means.
12. *Miracles*: The gift of miracles is the special ability that God gives to certain members of the Body of Christ to serve as human intermediaries through whom it pleases God to perform powerful acts that are perceived by observers to have altered the ordinary course of nature.
13. *Discerning of spirits*: The gift of discerning of spirits is the special ability that God gives to certain members of the Body of Christ to know with assurance whether certain behavior purported to be of God is in reality divine, human or satanic.
14. *Tongues*: The gift of tongues is the special ability that God gives to certain members of the Body of Christ (a) to speak to God in a language they have never learned and/or (b) to receive and communicate an immediate message of God to His people through a divinely-anointed utterance in a language they have never learned.
15. *Interpretation*: The gift of interpretation is the special ability that God gives to certain members of the Body of Christ to make known in the vernacular the message of one who speaks in tongues.
16. *Apostle*: The gift of apostle is the special ability that God gives to certain members of the Body of Christ to assume and exercise general leadership over a number of churches with an extraordinary authority in spiritual matters that is spontaneously recognized and appreciated by those churches.

17. *Helps*: The gift of helps is the special ability that God gives to certain members of the Body of Christ to invest the talents they have in the life and ministry of other members of the Body, thus enabling the person helped to increase the effectiveness of his or her spiritual gifts.
18. *Administration*: The gift of administration is the special ability that God gives to certain members of the Body of Christ to understand clearly the immediate and long-range goals of a particular unit of the Body of Christ and to devise and execute effective plans for the accomplishment of those goals.
19. *Evangelist*: The gift of evangelist is the special ability that God gives to certain members of the Body of Christ to share the gospel with unbelievers in such a way that men and women become Jesus' disciples and responsible members of the Body of Christ.
20. *Pastor*: The gift of pastor is the special ability that God gives to certain members of the Body of Christ to assume a long-term personal responsibility for the spiritual welfare of a group of believers.
21. *Celibacy*: The gift of celibacy is the special ability that God gives to certain members of the Body of Christ to remain single and enjoy it; to be unmarried and not suffer undue sexual temptations.
22. *Voluntary poverty*: The gift of voluntary poverty is the special ability that God gives to certain members of the Body of Christ to renounce material comfort and luxury and adopt a personal life-style equivalent to those living at the poverty level in a given society in order to serve God more effectively.
23. *Martyrdom*: The gift of martyrdom is the special ability that God gives to certain members of the Body of Christ to undergo suffering for the faith even to death while consistently displaying a joyous and victorious attitude that brings glory to God.

24. *Hospitality*: The gift of hospitality is the special ability that God gives to certain members of the Body of Christ to provide open house and warm welcome for those in need of food and lodging.
25. *Missionary*: The gift of missionary is the special ability that God gives to certain members of the Body of Christ to minister whatever other spiritual gifts they have in a second culture.
26. *Intercession*: The gift of intercession is the special ability that God gives to certain members of the Body of Christ to pray for extended periods of time on a regular basis and see frequent and specific answers to their prayers to a degree much greater than that which is expected of the average Christian.
27. *Exorcism*: The gift of exorcism is the special ability that God gives to certain members of the Body of Christ to cast out demons and evil spirits.

OTHER BOOKS BY C. PETER WAGNER

The Condor of the Jungle (with Joseph S. McCullough; Fleming H. Revell Co.)

Defeat of the Bird God (William Carey Library)

Latin American Theology (Wm. B. Eerdmans Publishing Co.)

The Protestant Movement in Bolivia (William Carey Library)

An Extension Seminary Primer (with Ralph Covell; William Carey Library)

Our Corinthian Contemporaries (Zondervan Publishing House)

Frontiers in Missionary Strategy (Moody Press)

Church/Mission Tensions Today (editor; Moody Press)

What Are We Missing? (Creation House)

Stop the World, I Want to Get On (Regal Books)

Your Church Can Grow (Regal Books)

Our Kind of People (John Knox Press)

Your Church Can Be Healthy (Abingdon)

Strategies For Church Growth (MARC)

Church Growth And The Whole Gospel (MARC)

Leading Your Church To Growth (MARC)

How To Have A Healing Ministry Without Making Your Church Sick (Monarch)

Index